VERSES OF V

CW01664468

C.P. BROWN

ZINC READ

Published by
This edition copyright © 2023 by Zinc Read
Design and setting By Zinc Read
Email- zincread@gmail.com
ISBN-978-93-5858-581-0

This is being sold on the condition that it cannot be used commercially or in any other form without the written prior permission of the publisher. They cannot be republished or sold or rented. And it cannot be operated among readers in bookbinding or any other form. All these conditions will also apply to the buyer of the book. All rights of copyright are reserved in this context. The contents of this edition have been taken from material available in the public domain. The View's and characters expressed in the books are of the author and his/her imagination and do not represent the views of publisher.

CONTENTS

PREFACE TO VEMANA

This author has attained great celebrity in his own country and in the adjacent parts of India; some information regarding his country and language may however be acceptable to the reader.

Telugu is a principal language of the peninsula of India. It is ancient; and has been highly cultivated. The nation of the Telugus was in former times very powerful, and its princes gave considerable encouragement to literature. The works of its ancient poets are numerous and very voluminous. It possesses a very scientific grammar, and a system of prosody nearly as highly polished as that of the Greeks. In this and some other respects the language is acknowledged to be more difficult than Sanscrit.

It is peculiarly smooth and elegant in its sound, and the poets have cautiously preserved its euphony. Hence Europeans have called it the Italian of India. The student may at first think this remark, which is no new one, unfounded; as the pronunciation is strong and decided; and as the mixture of Sanscrit terms often gives it a degree of roughness. But the pure rustic dialect as well as that of the poets is altogether different from this colloquial language; in the pure dialect most of those Sanscrit words that had harsh sounds are softened till they are as smooth and melodious as pure Telugu.

With Sanscrit it is closely connected; as closely as English is with Latin. But at the same time it is as truly original and nearly as copious as English. Like English it has borrowed its scientific terms from another tongue; and these Sanscrit additions are daily increasing. Thus the language is becoming less pure.

During the eighteenth century, the incursions of the Mohamedans effectually crushed the literature of Telangana; it has fallen low; and the colloquial dialect has become equally corrupt--men are now rarely met with among them who can read or explain the classical authors of the language; a knowledge of prosody is yet more rare.

Twenty five years of peace in Telangana under the British government have now afforded opportunities for some revival of literature. The establishment of the Honourable Company's College at Madras, and the encouragement there held out to good scholars in the language may have effected some revival; but much remains yet to be done. No poem or classical composition in Telugu has hitherto been printed; and I believe no translation of a classic into English has been attempted.

It now remains to give some account of my author, VEMANA, whose writings are peculiarly useful to those who study the language, the style being simple, and the variety of topics very extensive. These adages exemplify thousands of words inadmissible into more dignified poetry. The thought and connection are often abstruse while the terms used are quite familiar.

Of his history, little is known. He was not a Bramin but a *Capoo*, or farmer; a native of the Cuddapa district and born, I believe, in the neighbourhood of Gandicotta. He lived in the beginning of the eighteenth century. It is said that in verse 707 he has fixed the date of birth which is believed to have been his own. This date coincides with A. D. 1652. The date is given in the cycle of sixty years; but which cycle is intended is unknown. Many verses, however, prove satisfactorily that he wrote in the latter part of the seventeenth century when the Mohamedans were governors of that part of India. His family was powerful, but he renounced the world and became a *sanyasee* or ascetic. He calls himself a *Yogee*.

These verses communicate hardly any idea of his history or connections, and like all solitary ascetics (*sanyasees* or *yogee*) he has dropped his family name--calling himself simply Vema or Vemana at pleasure. This solitary life has led him to address all the verses to himself, which, if this be not recollected, certainly looks like the grossest egotism. This practice is far indeed from being peculiar to Vemana.

[The name Vema and Vemana do not appear to be used by the Telugus of the present day. Vema or Vemana in Sanscrit signify a loom. (see Wilson's Sanscrit Lexicon, page 854, and the Sabdartha Calpataru Vol. II, page 199). I believe these names to have been practical titles alone, without a definite meaning. Thus it is well known that the titles or names of Dante and Hafiz were not the original names of those poets; the first of whom was named Durante or Durando (see preface to Cary's Dante) and the second Muhammed Shemsuddin].

These poems have attained very great popularity and parts are found translated into Tamil and Malayalam or Canarese. Their terse closeness of expression sometimes renders them difficult to translate with elegance; but such passages exemplify the manly force of a language that in the common dialect is often weak and verbose.

Of his aphorisms many have become common proverbs. Parts of them are evidently close translations from Sanscrit works, particularly the *Hitopadesa* and *Bhagavat Gita*. In a few of these every word is pure Sanscrit.

Vemana was evidently, in philosophy, of the Vedanta school, a disciple of Vyasa, whom Sir William Jones has (in the Asiatic Researches, Vol I, page 362) entitled the Plato of India. With the mystic tenets of Plato, those of Vemana closely correspond while his moral doctrines as closely answer to those of Democritus.

These verses are chiefly of three classes: moral, satirical and mystic In the morals, many verses occur, breathing a spirit of devotion truly extraordinary in a Hindu. The satirical part is chiefly directed against the national religion and customs particularly against Bramins. None of it is personal. The mystic portion is chiefly of use as exemplifying the powers of the language. The reveries contained in this chapter are of a strangely abstruse nature and furnish a remarkable instance of a powerful mind searching for the light of truth which is lost in the darkness of heathen ignorance. The style of this and some other parts renders it easier to translate the verses into Latin than into English. I have, however, left none in Latin (aliess) that appeared to deserve an English one. To the more difficult verses I have subjoined a Telugu interpretation For some parts of this comment written in Telugu, I am indebted to two very learned Bramins who taught me the language, its grammar and prosody. They are Tippabhotla Venkata Siva Sastri of Masulipatnam and Advyta Brahmia, the Pandit belonging to the court in which I have the honour of being assistant judge.

To the mystic portion I have appended such notes as appeared requisite. Further elucidations of the most ample nature will be found in the Bhagavat Gita, with Dr. Wilkins's commentary and in Sir William Jones's essay on the Mystical poetry. Poetry of the East appears in the third volume of the Asiatic Researches; It would be easy to refer to many other authors; but to save the reader trouble in an enquiry that can gratify nothing but curiosity, I have subjoined a short explanation of the system.

Most of the Verses in Vemana are written in a *ataveladi* metre which consists of four lines; but the fourth line, with some exceptions, is a mere refrain or chorus in these words--*Viswadabhirama Vinura Vema*.

It is perhaps impossible to meet with a complete copy of this poet in a manuscript of any antiquity. The principal sources from which this edition is compiled are nine. These were collected from Bellary, Cuddapa Madras,

Vijagpatnam, and the city in which I wrote. Few of these copies contain above five hundred verses, none came up to seven hundred. The number, however, that I have succeeded in collecting is 2,100.

Of the state of the manuscripts, it is not easy to give a correct idea. Errors of the grossest nature in orthography, metre and rhyme deface every line; and erroneous words are substituted to elicit a sense that the transcribers thought proper to prefer. Thus they have eluded many of the difficulties in thought or expression; and the corruption is indescribable in verse.

Vemana having written the *tadbhava* word *guramu* (for gruhamu) a house, the copyists in defiance of metre and meaning have *gurramu*, a horse.

To remedy such errors I prepared a general index to my manuscripts, showing the place each verse occupies in each copy. For the verses in no two copies had the same arrangement. By this aid, the true reading has, I hope, seldom been lost. the correct metre I trust never--the most frequent corruptions were substitutions of Sanscrit terms in defiance of measure, for pure Telugu expressions.

To the remarks on mystic philosophy, I have subjoined a short explanation of Telugu prosody. The statements are taken from the *Bheemana Chandassu*, but the arrangement and mode of explanation are my own. Sir William Jones has remarked (As. Res 1-XVII on Panini) that "since grammar is only an instrument, and not the end of true knowledge, there can be little occasion to travel so rough and gloomy a path." To teach myself The science, I was obliged to reduce the rules given by Bheemana in a very fantastic from to their real import; and a mode then occurred to me through which by degrees I learnt the whole with care. The original is so mysteriously complex that the failure of most aspirants even among Bramins to a knowledge of prosody is not surprising.

C. P. Brown

23rd Nov., 1824.

* * *

1-99

To the sainted Bards, to the nine poets, to the Siva creed, to his essence, and to the boon-granting Gem, to those who attend in the heaven of Siva, to the god himself and to thy teacher--pray for aid of Vema.

1

The unborn (see 556) the slayer of *sharabha* endowed with the qualities of Siva and the lord of a thousand millions of demigods; the servants of Siva who sitteth at the root of the sacred Banyan, He that is endowed with the mind of Siva, the sage Somasekhara is my teacher.

[He who is exalted above mortality, the vanquisher of the *Chinmaya* full of blessedness, Lord of ten thousand millions of saints who is also devoted to Siva, this is he who dwelleth under the sacred Fig tree whose heart is enwrapt in bliss, the crescent crowned Teacher, that is, the Deity alone was my instructor].

2

Who ever learneth the verses uttered by the sainted, this man shall attain to that object which is emphatically Incomprehensible.

3

Shall not they who read the thousand verses uttered by the venerable Vemana (who is full of the divine nature) relinquish all filthy lure whether of mind or body. (For పదివి I have substituted భవిని the name given by Jangams to all persons and things that are not consecrated to the Jangam creed.)

4

He that will become a sage, and with pure faith learn these thousand verses without quitting them surely the place of beatitude is put into the palm of his hand.

5

That wise man who will even learn only the number of hundred verses, his appetites shall be at an end--and he by the four paths shall verily attain the abode of the Deity.

6

Know that the mind is the universal cause. By viewing and meditating on this, a man shall himself become spirit wherever he dwelleth all his days--know well the truth of this Vema!

7

Is it in the hand of any one to attain beatitude except that perfected saint who has himself become a portion of the universe? Though those roam the whole earth, the caverns, the mountains or the waters of the great deep?

8

The learned Brahmins who read all that is to be read, cannot yet attain heaven and the chief God. If you remain still without moving thy lips, this shall thee within thy mind, the glory of the perfected saint.

9

Perfect that the prime root is the first of beings whom it is out of our power to make known. If with our secret soul and the thought of our mind we meditate upon this perfect, then in the end of thine shall our whole living spirits attain beatitude. Therefore will Vemana even in his songs sings the preaches of this blessed power whose form he beholdeth in the chamber of his heart.

10

These worlds are all like leaves veiling the branch which is hidden from the view even of Brahma. He alone who can perceive the branch can sing its praises.

11

Though called yet remain silent; Though even again called yet maintain silence, whatever they think, or any one say, let the wise smile as though it was not intended for them; let them meditate in their souls on the supreme, hereby becoming themselves Eternal. The hermit that thus persistingly learneth shall like Vemana for ever attain the form of God.

12

One man became diseased, one became a donor every where, another became a possessor--such a man became a true saint. One himself became a libertine. But nowhere shall we see a mighty sage like to thee O Vemana--truly all these various forms pertain to thee O brother.

13

Agreeably to the character of an ascetic relinquish all the objects of carnality (or passion). Touch not carnal objects after the manner of a magnanimous sage on earth, consider them the offspring of carnality. Vema hath learned, to subdue all carnality.

14

Vemana openeth not his mouth to say no to anyone's assertion. Thus he seems like to a mad man. He can explain every mystery of that Vedantam which destroys all distinctions and differences. From this knowledge his apathy arises.

15

The worshipful teacher who by the due performances of worship hath attained merit. He by that worship shall see (i.e., obtain). Never shall he be changed.

16

By freely bestowing gifts you on one hand attain heaven but if you trust to your own mind delusion enters. Trust to the light of wisdom to destroy all that is inimical.

17

He whom in this world knows wisdom to him, there was no next world (he is as if in heaven). He shall not lose his soul even in the death of Brahma, In that he shall be absorbed in the divine mind.

18

Is he whom you call God in another land? With *Devee* (the Goddess) he is in the body. Mounting his vehicles (the senses), he rapidly drives his chariots.

19

Until you find the thing you have lost, you require a light--only so long--after finding it why keep the light? After becoming God why retain the body.

20

If thou fall at the feet of the teacher will the dog of passion seize ye thee? If you leave the teacher's feet, those dogs will seize thee. Indeed the dog's disposition does not attach to the teacher.

21

By knowledge of the great spirit he himself became all things. By the knowledge of life he became living. Let us first attain the destruction of love and opinion?

22

Why should ye in so many ways take care of (afford nourishment) this body? Will it not perish (go)? If knowing futurity ye purge away your impurities putting an end to destructions ye shall attain beatitude.

28

The cat having caught a muskrat delights not in it; but pursues the fowl to seize it. Without relinquishing the delights (possession) will love cease?

24

The only god is Eternal; to him who knows that all things curiously compounded are in truth the unity and afflictions are as a lie and to him beatitude is easy of attainment.

25

Again by perfection ghee is produced from curds, fire in trees, fragrance from fine flowers and oil in seeds; thus shineth forth god the soul of intellect.

26

By friction and friction fire is produced in a tree. By continual agitation ghee is produced in curd. Thus by perpetual meditation shall divine wisdom be produced in our body.

27

Until he explores his own soul, a man acts (or roams) in ignorance of God (or illusion caused by God). If by meditation you comprehend that God is a spirit by understanding the beatitude shall be clearly manifested to thee O Vemana.

28

This ignorant soul (living creature) after living so long imagines that to die and be reproduced is the course of nature. To know that heaven where we shall be so far advanced as to forget instruction this is spirituality. (Brahman)

29

Fire can even exist in a tree. But a tree has no power to remain where fire is. Like to fire in a tree, is the worldly state, It contains hidden the seeds of flame,

30

If a cloud intervenes in a way destroys the sun. if your inclinations intervene they destroy your firmness. If forgetfulness takes place it destroys beatitude itself

31

Consider the soul in its fourth state (the *turyavastha* or death); view it minute as a mote (cucumber-prickle). Hereby cut off all attachment to earthly desires. He who comprehendeth the essence (or savour) of wisdom, go to, he is Divinity.

32

Though he searches, he cannot see the teacher of wisdom (vedanta). There is none in the world who can discover truth, even he be found he will not look to any other object.

83

He that cloth not wallow in nor seek the enjoyments of sensual objects, who (in the earth) sees the path of obtaining those objects who yet calls all those deceptive pleasures which proceed from sensual objects sensuality, they are the wise. They enjoy this world declaring they enjoy it not.

34

The great teacher is concealed in the word. The teacher is the Essence of the word. The teacher is hidden in darkness. The teacher is the support of all.

35

Action and inaction are the same to him who sports with his acts and to him who is mighty in *tatwa*. If thou understand it from a determination of what is right (*dharmam*) and what the contrary and with pure mind truly set it forth.

36

They who are not able to free them from the trio of attachment (to sons, wife and wealth) shall remain plunged in the multitude of desires. How shall they attain the bliss of beatitude?

37

The senseless body (lit. animal) continueth for a while dies, and is reproduced in the course of nature. So know that mansion of absorption where thou shall forget knowledge. This is Divinity.

38

It is the favour of the excellent teacher and through much study that is illumed with knowledge and (good conduct) ethics, that shall put thee into right path. Teach men that the excellent teacher is himself a part of the Divinity.

39

If thou have not lost shame thou shall not attain the delight of god; unless thou humble and incline thyself shame will not leave thee. He who hath given all shame shall live a lengthened age (i.e., a man to be perfect must be independent of opinions).

40

Surely thy mother is thy wife and thy wife thy mother. Wise is he who has comprehended this regarding these two (incomplete).

41

Unless thou give up thy lusts thou shall not be released from thy ties. (lit. cord: earthly ties). Unless thou be free thou at no devotee. None but a devotee can be freed from all desires.

42

If you listen and listen to the voice within thy soul, the first saint shall not be entangled in desires. If thou attain light In the soul, this beatitude,

43

Convert thy mind into a fair chamber built in a summer mansion (pleasure house) with a bath, well and garden. Prepare it for meeting the maid of wisdom in secret and enjoying her charms. Thus let thy hours sweetly glide away.

44

If thou search in the place where a thing is, thou shalt find it. Why search in a place where it is not? Without the conjuration of deep thought thou canst not attain that thing that is above all desirable.

45

How did he learn all the truth, and yet fail of becoming the Eternal; carefully ascertaining the mystic word in abstraction, they distribute instruction regarding the wondrous from. (loose version).

46

In the flame of fire when thou hast firmly immolated (as a holocaust) all personal affection fixing thy thought on the unborn, this shall he an acceptable dedication to Hari.

47

Though fire is produced in a tree, is the tree conscious of that fire? Like as the fire is concealed in the tree, thus can no one perceive the nature of the devotee who hath dispelled those passions that harass the soul.

48

To gaze and gaze on the firmament in the mundane egg shall be excellently sweet to the sage if he fully meditates on it: abundantly blessed shall he be in whatever direction he directs his view or his steps.

49

How can he be a (Brahmin) Divine who knoweth not (Brahma) the Divinity in the city of the Divine egg or universe? To understand by own mind, go to, this is (Brahminity) Divinity.

50

The science taught by a teacher is known to the teacher. The teacher knoweth what the teacher explaineth. The power of the teacher is known to the primal teacher.

51

Understanding well in thy mind uniting thyself with thy mind and seizing him who is in thy mind--he that can stay his mind, this is the *yogee* who knows the great secret.

52

Ignorant that he is himself the truth (*tatwa*) he loves delusion which he imagines to be truth. If truly he sought for uprightness and virtue (*dharma and carma*) this should be, to him, the truth, that is the source of happiness,

53

He who constantly, without intermission, holdeth the all pervading Divinity in (the place of) his soul, he shall arrive at the ineffable dwelling, he shall truly comprehend the world--this is the truth.

54

Quitting this thick darkness of ignorance he who in due time forgetteth himself, and who fixeth his mind with care on the supreme, this great noble sage no where is to be found.

55

As when one sees a rope and mistakes it for a snake he is alarmed, but when he knows it is a rope his fear is over. Thus only when fear departs, can we know the true nature of god.

56

The Divinity appears diversely to all those who look him. They who seeing see and see him with understanding shall behold him; they themselves shall become that vision and that vision, them.

57

He who comprehends the creed of the spine (*cundali*) what hath that sage of might to do with the embraces of a girl --nobly in this body shall the maid of beatitude alone shine.

58

The Veda taught by Vemana is known to him alone. Hear! Others know it not. To those who understand Vemana shall the one letter (Om) be a thousand times taught and permanently impressed on their mind.

59

The corporal form being burnt in the flame of wisdom the body is all vexed crushing all that desire, that (rolls about or) is afflicted in the body. If thus we behold God, this is beatitude, O Vema!

60

He is like to a meditator, like a dumb man, like to an enjoyer, like a diseased one. He who knows every state shall become Omniscient and be like the prince of *yogees.*

61

Is not there one man living of good position? He may live some days in comfort. After living, living and living he lives no longer. If he will know the path to happiness, let him seize that stout thief, his mind cut into pieces and prepare a dwelling for himself in heaven.

62

What is the wisdom of that man who in the house of the body cannot distinguish his friends and foes? On him who knoweth them shall Divine ambrosia be bestowed.

63

Like as water flows in its channel thus does an immersion in that knowledge of truth that arises in the mind ultimately (through an absorption in the final essence) constitute the perfect saint. Then is he like to the Ganges when her streams reach the ocean. (a correct version of awful intricacy).

64

Casting away the mind and turning it back knowing the secret of the heart and if thou fix thy mind, this is the greatest task of religion.

65

While pride of the body remains, love and the lust plunge us in the ocean of reproduction. Therefore, desire, mental enemies, senses, thoughts, deceit and fraud are all like to dream let us awake O Vema!

66

If you comprehend not the entire secret and if thy mind be not bound up to one aim, the Divine secret shall not be revealed to thee. Should it be shewn openly it would be but as the unveiling of the secret parts.

67

If we look into these our bodies let us with inner vision consider that the nature our forms possess is also that of all other bodies--with devotion do all penitents, behold this.

68

If the teacher knows not in his character, the prime teacher, he is himself as blind. The teacher who teaches the teacher is the lord of life.

69

If first thy intellect steadfastly attached to thy resolution, it shall dissipate this blind sleep. If this sleep be dissipated, it shall cause thee to attain fearlessness. By tranquillity thou shalt gain the assemblage of all felicity. By that felicity thou shall become the whole world. By being united to the universe thou shalt become divine essence. By subduing thy senses, the essence (permanent life) shall remain stable in thee. If thou thus fix the divine essence, thou shalt become it. By becoming the lord of the kings of saints thou shalt shine brilliantly; thou shalt walk in delight and with deliracy like an infant, like to an aged man, like a spirit (nocturnal apparition) like a mad man shalt thou be. Behold thus, shalt thou act in thy dignity.

70

Whatever there be of knowledge and ignorance in the mind, we can neither perceive, see nor hear it. If we attempt to take hold on the mind to seize and bind it we shall see that the body is replete with delusion and nothing but delusion.

71

Though we know delusion to the death we cannot quit it in the courts of God. They cannot see his equals and co-equals. Were all mighty would there be a distinguished place for God?

72

All this life is illusion; possession and connections are delusion; understanding is delusion. I myself on consideration, am delusion. He that understands this illusion is the sage that comprehends the great secret.

73

They know not the secret that this is all a world of delusion. They are entangled in delusion and deluded. If you only understand this delusion you shall attain the celestial regeneration.

74

Wives and sons are delusion; connections are delusion; wealth and greatness are delusion; the body is delusion, he that is aware of this delusion is the sage who knows all secrets.

75

Born in delusion, grown in delusion to what end is a man who cannot discern the nature of delusion. He who can understand this delusion is the only happy man in the world.

76

For the sake of delusive worldly state, a man being ensnared in it wanders in delusion, After he understands this delusion through delusion itself he attains beatitude; that is, his sins, by his quitting them, become sources of felicity.

77

As long as we are held in the present delusion, the abode of the true state (of perfection) is beyond our reach. Then let us become perfected in accomplished essence.

78

When we see our true figure shall we see truly that our body is born of delusion. He alone who beholdeth within himself the possession of the truth, this is the *parama yogi*.

79

The delusion of delusion is the great *maya*; the *maya* that hath not suffered delusion is unknown; it exists not. The *maya* that is not delusion is truth.

80

(Mystic) If through pleasure, and the favour of the teacher, if thou quit this house with nine doors, thou shalt become the universal spirit and the universe.

81

Strife ceases when anger ceases; when strife ceases wishes also cease. The connections that lead to future transmigrations cease when distinctions are done away and when the three qualities of virtue, passion and ignorance are dissolved, beatitude is permanent, O Vema.

82

He that knows not the mystical syllable, Om, never can become a saint. He that knows not the glory of god is no *yogee*. He that knows not the everlasting is not in a state of beatitude.

83

By conquering the senses he that is steady knows the essence of god. How should a man not knowing himself will call such a man a sage?

84

He who daily and highly considers and forgets from his mind the distinctions of I and thou and he that thus liveth is the noble ascetic.

85

Search and view thyself; thou art the living being. Behold the great (*tatwa*) existent and thou shalt become the spirit. Earth and Heaven shall depart and delusion herself be destroyed.

86

He who knowing all the powers of Him who dwelleth in the dwelling shall seize his evil mind and seat it. He who can retain his body is the greatest of devotees.

87

If thou apply thy heel and hold it firmly to thy anus and then seek for thy interior so as to understand the entrance of power, then if thou also cause a change in thy mind (give thy word) and determine on attaining felicity and it becomes the perfection. This is the path of perfection (or *yoga*).

88

By aid of the observances the mind is stayed. By wrath it is dissipated. The steadfast mind obtains fearlessness. Resolution puts an end to alliance. The mind that is removed from alliance suffers us to attain tranquillity. From tranquillity is equality he himself becomes the entire world. If he be transmuted into the universe, he is Essence (*tatwa*). That Essence will watch its opportunity and vanquish all the senses. If he becomes thus skilled in *tatwa* he shall become it himself. He shall thus be a *raja yogi* in lustre and shine in the world.

89

Words are a pack of evils; to keep a matter secret is a virtue; avarice is like to death, loan a misfortune, an oath is an evil, words are arrows--all this is not in the least known to men.

90

Why does this body a bag with nine holes in it, require convenient things and a high caste, tell me. Believe not that it is thine. Understand and say I am Brahma,

91

All men are intoxicated and entangled in the six inimical causes of evil propensities. Imagining this to be the path of prudence they walk in it; but they cannot view and perceive the truth of god.

92

Burning the tree of earthly ties, the wise man engaging himself in wisdom proceeds with propriety. The tree thus burnt will be very delightful.

93

Seeing that connections keep the world in darkness, connections yet form a tie between man and his creator. If all these connections were dissolved, then in the true path should man see beatitude. (Loose version)

94

The eye is first fixed on the path of instructions. In the midst, when we have learned somewhat the view dwelleth on our own mind, and at the last the vision resteth on him who is pure light.

95

Whenever you behold him he is looking at nothing else; he fixes his eyes with quivering lids upon beatitude night and day in one fixed manner, shall he ever learn to bow to Yama who visiteth the sins of men? What more need we say the whole way of beatitude shall be attained by Vemana.

96

Unless thou relinquish vain words, the formula (of prayer and worship) cannot be learnt; unless thou relinquish the form of prayer and become absorbed in meditation the mind cannot be restrained. Unless thou restrain thy mind thou shalt not attain beatitude.

97

In this filled vessel of the body with which light and darkness agree well, if we forget the sleep of meditation, however great we be we cannot know the first thing.

98

He that will strive and bind all the designs, or think not on anything in his mind, but be like as a picture, this is the truly great man, whether he be in forest or town,

99

He who will remain in contemplation with quivering eyelids and fail not to fix the Being in his mind, but perpetually view him--easy is not anywhere for beatitude to be duly placed in him.

* * *

100-199

100

By mere thinking shalt) thou attain truth? If thou meditate not, but remain still shalt thou reach it? By thinking neither on thought nor on the absence, this is true path and beatitude.

101

If thou fix the sight of both thy eyes equally and thy mind he similarly fixed, if thou restrain all external tastes and heedfully gaze, the deity shall be made evident to thee.

102

Closing the external nine and mingling the internal airs with your mind, if, understanding this secret you perform the worship of the (*atmalingam*) Divinity, this is the beatitude.

103

Let the pure saint confuse all his connections (valenu for valenu) in this outward world in conformity to his high desires. In his outward connections be thus dissolved he shall attain heaven and beatitude (*Kailasa and Mukti*) .

104

Quickly stop your anus with your left heel and fasten your anus and part of generation. Then set thy desire in thy mind on the unseen (secret) and behold him.

105

He whose mind sleeps in abstraction is the great saint wherever he lies, the securest situation is the (destruction) retention of respiration. He who can securely loose his apertures (*mudras*) they being fixed of themselves becomes the chief. He is not entangled in connections; is alone the independent sage. (lit: Indifferent) 106

He who maketh his inmost mind pure (or who maketh his inside his outside) and slays all worldliness, burneth his caste and casting off all qualities hath attained the reflection of reflections. He is the devotee.

107

If thou truly understand, thou cannot seek god. Then can't see him if thou move not thy eyeballs. If thou wink not thy eyelids, he will appear betwixt them.

108

He who fixing his view eagerly on the end of the nose, looking into his heart, hath noble might. If he knows the path of beatitude, h becomes the exalted devotee.

109

The spirit that is named unparalleled being united with the spirit of his pristine name will be destroyed in one mode. That mode Vemana will teach thee.

110

He who has severed the desires of his house from him and duly in his heart is cautious; he who thus establishes his house, is deeply skilled in tatwa.

111

He is the happiest person in the world who in whatever his views and in the six creeds and sects and the four *asramas* wavers not at any time in his walk.

112

It is impossible for us to see the wondrous writing on the noble hill in our path, following the shadow of our nose. If we go to view, it is perfection. It is Siva.

113

A man shall attain long life when he has learnt to low breathing (*i.e.* to save up some respirations daily of the portion predestined to each man). Then shall he grow, he shall wear his body through out the age of Brahma.

114

He that will not be entangled in the forest of (*acshara*) letters but considering the (nobleness) charms of (*acshara*) the indestructible, and in this earth adores the prime letter (*Om*) this man shall become Imperishable (*acshaya*). This is sufficient!

115

There is no distinct region named deity; self is evidently the deity. If thou know thyself thou art the divinity.

116

The whole world exists in the divine atom. The divine atom lies hid in our body The man that restrains his mind will surely attain beatitude (*mucti*).

117

Like him who, holding butter in his hand, but not knowing its properties, wishes for ghee (which he might obtain by merely melting the butter) is he who being himself divinity meditates on God as though removed from him.

118

By beholding the first of being thou shalt become united with the universe. No man is able to behold that prime existence. That prime who is the path of bliss existeth within the soul.

119

He who knows clearly in his own mind that he is a part of the universe, internally and externally, the man who hath brightly learned this shall in this world attain beatitude.

120

By not knowing clearly the corporal frame that exists in the external frame, those that are without become outcast. To know that external that is within this external--this is Divine knowledge.

121

All matter is concreted in the world and all is again resolved into space. That which we call the Divinity if we comprehend it, beatitude shall be manifested to us.

122

If thou make the face of the heaven and thy own face to be one and manifest the true nature of the external figure of the divinity, thou shalt by knowing outward external attain bliss. (loose version, the original being more obscure).

123

All connections are produced in this world; they are not aboriginal; and those ties shall again be resolved into primordial matter--view this well, if these connections be doomed to become resolved into space, then the path to beatitude is found to be in void (paraphrase).

124

The god knows him who is in the eye pupil: behold in the sky, Him who is in the pupil. The eye and the sky become the sky of the heart.

125

A man must become eternal by knowing the source of truth; and learning carefully the inmost word (the signification of the scriptures or *upanishads*) consider who that word is and closely view it.

126

If thou know the five lettered name of Namassiva thou knowest the supreme! If thou know the supreme, thou shalt for ever shine. He who shines glorious becometh the Spirit.

127

If the unborn enters our inner man as we meditate, we shall attain beatitude, but never shalt thou attain it by gazing on external shapes.

128

If by holding the Linga we become resolved into primitive nature, gazing on our bodies, we shall be happy. But men will not know the signification of the Linga, and thereby attain that coalescence. (Observe this curious grammatical construction) 129

The teacher, the image of Siva, compounded the three worlds into one, and combined the six worlds; thus he remains firm (these nine worlds, or regions are the nine mystic *chacras* of the human form).

130

If, ignorant of the postures thou learn not of thy teacher, their secret force (*murma & curma*) and fix not thy heart how shalt thou become of the second birth? (*Dwija* signifying a Brahmin, means, reform-regenerate) 131

The body is the Mundane Egg; what is called soul is air. The eyes are the moon and sun in our estimation. Where is there a Divinity beyond this? Ye are gods in your own estimation.

132

We are born in air and grown in air. Understand the order of blessing in the air. For, from air is born that air of the soul which is our essence.

133

He who has himself become the universe and knows that the great whole dwells in him and who has learned to unite his inner man with all that is external this man while yet on earth, has attained perfection.

134

Meditate on the thought that is within our thought and know it; this thou must do in the appropriate mode by giving up all thy other thoughts. The thought of thought is essence (*tatwa*); it is soul (or it is the essential spirit).

135

Connection originates in this outward world. Let it be resolved again into universe. If we resolve it fairly into universe, this is the path to happiness.

136

If thou become the universe, the great all shall shine resplendent in thee, that man who knoweth the god who shineth within him shall hereby attain beatitude.

137

If thou canst see that the all is one, thou shalt attain a sure knowledge of God; thy eye-lid shall not close night or day. Behold that great spirit that is the light of light.

138

Unless thy outward form be (humbled) mortified thou shall not see the living form. But who is able to mortify that outward form? Unless the creation be destroyed, we cannot behold the creation.

139

All fear belongs to the body; If we quit fear the certainly we shall attain will be that of the great spirit; the only destruction shall be that of the body. Teach men that victory is the property of the soul.

140

The *yogee* who knows the one letter (Om) shall know the (*param*) Deity, beholding him and attain his nature. He shall himself become the forms in which the Deity exists and all the rest of the creation, becoming a particle of the primeval unity.

141

The *yogee* who raiseth his palms aloft fixeth his feet, fixeth his gaze full on heaven becometh hereby part of the universe and attaineth length of days.

142

Consider that fire, and air, and all worlds exist in the body at their proper places. Then touch and behold the Teacher in thy mind.

143

If thou quit not the hopes of the place above and devise a mode attain it, thou shalt arrive therein, that place and thou shalt be united, and thou shalt become the self-existent Deity.

144

He is himself metamorphosed into the worship and into the worshipper that performs adoration. He becomes himself sacrificial implement. Wherever he performs worship he becomes himself (Omnipresent). He is myself, and I myself am, he.

145

All that is born on the earth was born in the earth. All reality is born in the body. The great whole is produced from toil . Let us ourselves become that mighty whole.

146

If the soul be closely united with the body though it be devout, unless it quits, the body is not blessed. Through the body must we attain the abode of beatitude.

147

If thou know that the prime existent is single and fix thy mind on that prime, never quitting the prime thou shalt become the unborn. He that path quitted the prime is like to the blind.

148

Without making distinctions of situations (lit, without saying there or here) as we behold all things, the god (Vishnu) ever views and comprehends all things. The circumambient (God Vishnu) goes around the orbit of the world.

149

By considering forms thou shalt attain the unseen and thy form shall assimilate to his. Devoid of both these (i.e., body and mind) become thus invisible. (loose version)

150

By viewing thyself inwardly, thou shalt become the joy of the world. By viewing what is external, thou shalt be immersed in earthly connections. By beholding thyself, the divinity shall become thy salvation.

151

That divinity who is our rescue is attained by deep thought. If thou comprehend him by meditation thou shalt become that being, If thou know the thought of thought, thou shalt become it.

152

All those who possess pure wisdom gaze of the Mundane Oval. If thy mind be pure, thou shalt ever gaze on the admirable *pindanda* universe of the body.

153

Being born in a human generation and grown up in it, if, after becoming a man, a man cries scorn on the line of men, and (become a *Haracula*) becomes a participator in the nature of Siva; he shall become Siva.

154

The devotee who knoweth the great secret walketh with out considering the burning sunshine, he shall live to all time on the earth. Is the attainment of wisdom in the power of a glutton?

155

To nourish our bodies let us cease from all mental occupation and by the aid of the living being let us daily rove free from care. By considering our bodies, we shall perceive that the Divine soul permanently resides within us.

156

In the one body of the universe there are forms innumerable. How many forms shine in it! When they perish all shall become one whole. Thus is the nature of spirit. (This ataveladi has four versions).

157

(A difficult verse in pure Telugu)

It is only one man here and there who can try and explain the second birth of (*yatees*) the recluse with extreme exactitude. It is an extraordinary qualification; sense is more stable than even worship.

158

Where is heaven for that soul full of cupidity, that thinks his body is his own self and entangled in his own (vāsana, smell) attractions ensnared in repeated births and deaths. Ignorant of all matter wallows in lusts.

159

He who grips his foot in the palm of his hand and with an eye fixed on heaven stands firm. He shines transformed into the universe and shall live long.

160

Those voluptuaries who forget their thoughts and principles (i.e., themselves; lit. *chitta* is the faculty of doubt and *buddhi* that of assurance) are given up to vain confidence and cannot collect their whole attention and fix it on Siva. They shall never attain bliss (terribly difficult).

161

How should those who imagine themselves to be one with their body, and who remain immersed in the ocean of the cursed three attachments (to wife, son and wealth) attain the knowledge (*sangati*) of the truth (*moksham*).

162

He exists in the shape of the universe and is the general soul. He is the all witnessing spirit. He hath truly converted.. himself into the soul. Look at the universal world. He is himself all and even exists in truth.

163

He that has seen is greater than who has heard. But he that possesses Him is greater than who hath beheld. Greatest of the noble is he in the earth.

164

It thou firmly fix the idea of the divinity in the mind, and establish thyself in the temple of the body, thou shalt be firm in the earth and attain the inner vision.

165

If thou excuse that life (*jiva tatwa*) that possesses the marks of vitality, to be united to the teacher, he is greater than the life. He who thus restrains the body is himself.

166

The great whole exists within us. If we know that we are, if, by this means of salvation in this soul shall the man who thus walks attains heaven.

167

If a man be converted into his intrinsic self in the midst of all external he would contract no alienation. I swear by my father. If we were converted into self how should we entertain any anxiety?

168

If he be himself prudent cautiously will he save himself, and in every manner he considers himself as the great spirit.

169

If he knows that he is himself the universe and the universe himself; that he is himself all essence, if, knowing this he fails to walk accordingly, there is no salvation for that map.

170

(Pure Sanskrit) Water, earth, fire, sky, air--it is well known that these compose the world. The natural body, the invisible form, the body of delusion, if thought on, are the basis of all.

171

To say I will not this (i.e., wish not for it) and still not to leave it but remain entangled in the desire of things convenient nor quit them. This is origin of worldliness.

172

If the face and name are unalterable, the name and the face are both implicated in our acts. It would be well if we could lose both our name and face.

173

The devotee to Siva who understands all the properties of the body, shall not entangled in desire and deceived to his ruin. How should a juggler be ensnared by any man?

174

The exalted sages have declared in the earth that when through instruction a man relinquishes the desires (or schemes) of his mind, he shall through his love of them attain the abode of purities.

175

If thou be thyself excellent, but, as the bliss be wedded to nature and ruin thy beatification thou shall not behold that preceptor who caused the creation of precepts.

176

Doth an infant know any thing of (dressing) roasting stones to extract metals? The god-like sage alone comprehends it. Know thou the degraded nature metal and leave it?

177

If thy mortal form perish, thy inward eye shall clearly shine. If the fruits be destroyed that tree becomes free as the tree of desire. If thy eye be humbled to see with it is happiness.

178

Where is shame hidden? Where is the darkness of ignorance hidden? Where is hunger hidden? In the soul! Learn ye the hiding of the hidden sleep of abstraction.

179

Look on thy chief (jewels or foes) passions! Haste to destroy them nourish the whole of thy friends (or lovers). He who thus behold the great light and in the midst of the body fixes his desire--this man is himself Hari.

180

Our own shadow is our foe, and our shadow is a witness to us of our bulk in the body; my passions are my enemies and my mind is the only aid I have. This is true.

181

To cut off the evils (diseased) of the body ceasing the look of love towards the robbers (evil wishes) knowing the origin, attaching our thought to him and uniting the mind to him--If the devotee thus recognizes the (friendship) mutual love between the creature and the creator, this is the institute of sanctity.

182

Though the sage be touched (or affected) by any object of sense, he is not in truth moved truly. Vemana hath learnt, in the host of sensual objects and passions to abstain from the six evils (*cama, crodha, lobha, moha, mada, matsara*) and all other sources of sin (*durvishaya*). (a tremendous puzzle, but correctly done.) 183

If we consider our real form however great we may seem in our own delusions, and those of ascetics, and be filled with them can we hereby see god.

184

He that hath seen and can name the place of his primordial birth, walks in wisdom in the earth; the place of our origin is in the divinity (tatwa).

185

From fire which was produced from air was water created; in the atmosphere it appeared, being self born; such is the history of *Maya*, that had no father.

186

Those who in their minds muse on the gem on the summit of essence are skilled in *tatwa*. He who hath truly beheld in the midst of darkness, the great light, this is the devotee. He who truly knoweth that the soul exists in God and God in the soul hath religious vision. He is the pure, who in the*Sankhya yogamu* (which enumerates the qualities of spirit) hath ascertained that the entire world is in Siva. In any but this path shall any one ever attain the deity? If the life leave the belly, and depart how should it be puffed up?

187

If thou walk not so as to become free from. (set aside) all the evil qualities of thy acts how should thou acquire the divine essence? Will a lamp devoid of oil blaze merely by filling it with dry sesasum oil seeds--that are not freed from their hurtful substance.

188

Like as the seeds and the husk (between themselves) are born together in water but the husk (goes) is destroyed so the concomitant evil fruits of his acts who knows the essence of God will leave him undefiled--Indeed it is thus.

189

Acts of religion are far removed from the wise and the wise is far from acts in *Caliyuga*. The man of purity who ceaseth both works and knowledge truly hath attained beatitude, For, when he is perfect, faith and works shall both terminate.

190

If thou be not a performer of acts thou knowest not good works. He who is trueth to works shall not see any good. Unless thou enter the water, surely thou can't know the depth; nor, devoid of works know happiness.

191

If thou look upon the fruits of thy actions as being defiled will hypocrisy; then shalt thou attain the fruits of thy righteousness. Felicity consists in surpassing both thy righteousness and thy good works.

192

Fruits (senses) produced in a tree (the body) exulting, united in fair beauty, ripen--eat the fruits (beatitude) and know the leaves of a tree. (Here it is impossible to discriminate in English between *caya* and *pandu*).

193

Like as a swan will not touch the (*mansodakam*) heavenly stream but turns it off, thus let the yogee be untouched by acts; he shall ramble in all delight.

194

Searching well into the body and setting God before our eyes, and throwing aside our future acts, verifying our mind and quitting the love of our various ties, he that applies himself to stand there, is the best: 195

The *Puranas* of acts are a great deep. In those acts never shall we see Siva; surely none is able to declare Siva, the destroyer of acts. Acts are vile, and vile.

196

Vishnu, Brahma, the demigods, the *munis* and all the rest were nobly born and then lost their state of happiness, regularly proceeded through the state of decrepitude and death. This was through the savour of delusion.

197

They who perpetually enquire which among three Gods is the chief (or root) cannot, being fools, know the chief--surely there is a higher root of the three.

198

There are men who being unable first to perceive which is the noblest of the three, go into destruction. There is one original substance of which the three are formed.

199

Know ye (ascertain and learn) that root that knoweth the three. First know Him who is above the three and extol him with the tongue.

* * *

200-299

200

Every thing is called the act of deity. But there is a deity superior to this god. That god slew Vishnu and he destroyed the appearance of Siva (*abhava*) Surely this is the great God indeed if thou consider it well.

201

They call a pot, olla; they name a hill, collis; salt they call sal; are they not however one? The languages alone are diverse, the essence is one.

202

Vishnu, Siva, and Brahma all see the leaf but view it who will, none can perceive the branch. Were the branch behold, would any abstain from lauding it?

203

He, he, and he exist in him; neither he, he, nor he is He. He that unites them with him--go to--he is the Divinity.

204

If thou know the beauty of the five letters, in these five cloth beatitude consist. He (the divinity) is the one who dwells in that five.

205

Slay Brahma, and mingle him with Vishnu. Slay Vishnu and resolve him into Siva. Slay Siva and become thyself the Siva yogee (or chief spirit).

206

To them who understand the meaning of the excellent *sankhya yoga* I will in this world declare the truth through the most noble *raja-yoga*. Listen to the greatness of Siva (pure sanskrit).

207

Why all this grief. If with singleness of heart thou extinguish thy desires by immersing thy soul in (Hari, Hara and Aaja, Vishnu, Siva and Brahma) the three gods and maintain a subdued spirit, happiness shall be formed within thee.

208

The body of this visible world is a vessel of God, the life therein is air. The sun, moon and fire are his eyes (number, body assemblage of eyes). There is no God but this.

209

He who slays his great (five) foes, and vanquishes cupid, and has learnt the five lettered name (*Namassivaya*), he attains the porch of him, the five faced who is entitled *Bhava* (emphatically existence i.e., Siva).

210

Of what use is that Saiva faith that knows not the path through this universe compounded of inanimate and animate bodies and lingams, They shall not know the becoming (or the act of transformation into) Hara the eight bodied.

211

He who divideth the lord Iswara into seven parts and has dedicated by the ceremony of pouring his whole body to God by any unfailing practice of such conduct shall become the chief of yogees.

212

He who hath attained the bliss that dwells in the five lettered name, shall shine both here and hereafter in bliss. To know this life and next, this is deity.

213

Mighty let us to cut pieces the six and seven foes of our souls and in the defection of wisdom unless we worship the dwellings of the three gods how shall we attain happiness? The forehead mark, food and scars on the body and daubings with ashes are in vain applied. Can the sons of earth hereby attain bliss through the love of these? O Vemana, the noblest of princes?

214

If thou be thyself converted into those three Brahma, Vishnu and Siva, who created, saved and destroy the three worlds and praise them, this man shall be transformed into the deity.

215

He who hath reduced Brahma, Vishnu and Siva in one shall become a *parama yogee* and the divinity. How can we comprehend one who thus is equal to the divinity.

216

Those who will not cease from the radical bond of the root (the mind) unless they destroy the eight creeds, how should they be called sages, rather are they mad.

217

The lingam is the great Siva; the life of the body if that creature be purified he shall attain God. Were there two paths how could the deity be attained?

218

Seize the robbers (passions) and put them to death; spare but one (the mind) whoever he be that knows this secret, this shall be to him the fruit that he seeks.

219

Let us seize the four robbers (four lusts and smite them on the head, *cama*, *crodha*, *lobha* and *moha*) but spare one (the mind) to the men of the mind that they may attain the fruits of wisdom.

220

The man who hath learnt to view the order of the secret charms of the six and three temples, he shall attain the path to perfection. True is this doctrine.

221

If thou gain the favour of Siva and thereby destroy the first principle (*agnyana*) of thy tree (body) and cast it (ignorance) as its root (*maya*) and thus worship Siva, thou shalt be as a mountain and how should death befall thee?

222

Have you seen the three worlds, beheld and attained to the three objects that possess the three qualities and the beatitude that dwells therein?

223

He who looks upon rain, wind and sunshine as equal and abstains from thinking of honour or the like and continue in subjection--this is a stout hearted saint (yogee).

224

(The *Parabramham*) Under this tree there is not even the least shade; If the waters of delusion are unable to overflow this tree, it is as tree, how should that tree die?

225

(The power of delusion) Often in the midst of her reality shakes her head in scorn, she often laughs, she is no woman, what means woman? and What is the name of the being?

226

(mystic) When the five birds (passions) were found in their hole (the body) and cried, one of them sought the origin. The parrot that sought him became him.

227

If the unknown being by meditation appear in thy mind thereafter to say he is dead merely signifies his ultimate tie; when, thou die give up all earthy connections and worship (Sarvēsa) the Lord of all (total obscurity).

228

The words of Vemana, if soundly understood, are surely the essence of all the Vedas. If thou do not invite and comprehend thy greatness in the five-lettered name shalt thou enjoy prosperity?

229

Wisdom is the prime teacher to this whole world. The one *Pranava-mantra* is the original teacher (teacher of teachers) and thirdly, truly, the *Gayatri mantra* is the teacher of our actions.

230

If thou understand the mystic syllable '*Om*' (Pranava mantra) if it be in thy mind, the multitude of the acts of the mind shall not in the least affect thee. Then shall the devotee shine, a lamp of Divine knowledge.

231

Understand the power of the 'Om', Pranava mantra--it is the lingam. It resides in the three persons. Can others (those who are without) know and worship it?

232

He who hath united into one the composition of letters of the mystic syllable 'Om', and the visible mundane egg, he shall enjoy that letter 'Om'; and shall in certainty inherit bliss.

233

Why thou hast truly entered into the import of the mystic form of letters in 'Om' why persist in reading ten millions of other subjects? Fitly and visibly, shall the two letters Siva, constitute purity of soul in thee.

234

They who have rightly ordered their inner man, and considering justly the state of their heart, thrust it away, these are men of understanding. These shall dwell in delight in heaven--(terribly difficult).

235

They talk and talk of Divinity. What is in this Divinity? Were they to apply themselves and understand and see he is close to them. They cannot perceive the (*mudricas*) shadows that flit before the eyes closed in meditation.

236

The soul dwells in the little world of the corporal frame; and the sun inhabits the greater world of the universe and the divinity dwells in the sound, the globules of the splendour.

237

The fair (*nadam*) sound is produced from the (jyotee) visionary lights. The fair (bindu) globules are born from the nadam; and from the *bindu* are earth and heaven born.

238

All those who comprehending in their mind the scheme (or knack) of gazing at the sky (the khechari mudra) and who dispute not vainly these have subdued delusion. Can it other-wise be subdued?

239

The hooded serpent by knowing well to fix its gaze like as the crow under the cover gazes, thus does the yogee by inner wisdom gaze; this is the path of perfection.

240

How subtle is the interior vision? Pure is the sight of sight. Equal to the deity is the eye of our eye.

241

If thou carefully fix thy sight on the top of thy nose, then does a man correctly view the pre-eminent. He who hath known the pre-eminent cutteth off all secular ties.

242

Unless he sees (i.e., comprehend) the divine name (the mystic syllable named *Pranava*), a man cannot become faithful Unless he behold the lights (*jyotees*) that appear to the closed eyes, he is not in the way. Unless he behold the everlasting he is not in the state of beatitude.

248

By the *mudricas* in the mind being rightly ordered, as thou gazest on the *linga* of soul (the deity), it shall be manifested to thee and shall it be bestowed on thee devoid of teacher? That thou should'st understand it?

244

(Mystic) By gazing at the blight mudras, happiness or sorrow is produced. Looking at the blessing of the mudras and enjoying it, thou shalt shine as a beatified saint.

245

Unless thou dissolve the splendours of three affections, how should one attain permanent bliss in a fit manner? Unless thou annihilate thy mind can beatitude be put into thy hand, 246

Fixed in meditation, with eyes and ears closed, heard a ringing as of a bell in my mind; beholding I beheld a pure splendour and attaining the divinity. I beheld it within me. This is no hypocrisy. Look then to me.

247

Behold the (*bayalu-ācāsa*) sky and consider that splendour, view the departure of that light, uninjured. He that can view uninjured shall stand unshaken.

248

Lose not understanding behold the enlightening *calas*--confuse not the *calas* steadily behold the inner heaven (*bayalu-antarācāsa*); confuse not that heaven and steadily thou shalt behold the divinity.

249

In meditation if after gazing steadily thou persist not to the end, when thy sight fails again push on thy glance again. Him that fails unable to push it on, they look on as very light person.

250

Munees esteem the splendours that appear to the devotee fixed in meditation wonderful and excellent. If they understand, this is the chief spirit.

251

He is no exalted sage who cannot view the globules or his ringing sound, nor unite the splendours. Whatever pains he takes how shall he attain beatitude?

252

Let us know the time of attaining the truth and thus become the eternal. Let us thoroughly attain the mystic form (bindu) that exists with (lit. in) the sound (nadam). Then shall we attain bliss, and participate with no others in that enjoyment.

253

He that can convert the *nadam* into the *bindu* and into the *nadam* again, also convert the *nadu*, the *bindu*, and the *kala* into one (place) and perceive the sound, this man shall become the *yogee* full of bliss.

254

The devotee who knoweth the internal sound produced in meditation, shall with joy know the soul within him and attain felicity. That sound is the giver of beatitude, proclaim this for the consolation of all men.

255

The yogee who knows the sound (*nadam*) shall in his mind know the path described in the *vedanta* proclaim abroad that this sound is the means of beatitude.

256

Lose the idea of "mine and thine" and be illustrious in the belief of exalted abstraction (nadam). By the absence of the belief and disbelief, thou shalt attain prudence.

257

He who through instruction hath attained the (*nadam, the bindu* and *the kala*) ringing sound, the globules and the splendours, that he perceives who in meditation seals his eyes and ears, he who establishes these in his soul and well fixes his wandering mind, this is the mighty sage whose soul shall obtain its passage through the sagittal suture of the skull.

258

The saint who knoweth the (nadam) ringing sound shall know the indivisible God and the mystic syllable. That is the seed of the five charactered name (*Namassivaya*). Proclaim to men that the *nadam* in the mind is the beatitude.

259

Convert the *nadam* and *bindu* into one *nadam* and convert the nadam, the bindu and the kala into a single nadam, to meditate while beholding the nadam, this is perfection.

260

Consider what is the twenty sixth essence. It is a wondrous vital spirit. If thou unite it intimately with the chief spirit in the (*gurupada*) cerebral suture. Him who doth this they shall surely call saint.

261

Establishing the six gods in the six limbs and fixing the chamber of the head firm on the one pillar of the spine, the reckoning is to allow but one ruler (man) to each house.

262

There are six sustainers of the earth. There are the six rulers, princes of the earth. The noble and great warriors are these know that the body is their chariot and mark the result.

263

The divinity (*atma linga*) dwells in what is termed the *ajna chacra* (the space between the eyes). It is only by gazing intently on this part that shines so nobly, that beatitude shall be attained by men.

28 4

Cut down in thy soul the five chacras, nobly surmount those chacras and behold the plain beyond them.

265

The tree of beatitude has no (beginning) root but four fair boughs (forms of existence, animal, vegetable, insects, minerals). It is open to view and produces fruit. If thou eat them, they have no taste but cause appetite.

266

In that house in the threshold of which three ways meet with air, in the place where those three meet cloth Siva dwell (mystic of the body--worthless).

267

He who has the skill firmly to dwell in the six and three chacrams knowing their beauty he hath found the path to perfection.

268

If thou meditate in thy mind, in the sagittal suture shall there stand, He who is ruler of all to all who worship him does he give both sustenance and salvation.

269

Mind, words and works--if thou give up these three, and walk not up and down the royal path (a mystic part of the body), then shall any loss befall the yogee?

270

He who restraineth the six (lotuses) mortal parts of his body, and carefully fixeth his anus or backbone, and the parts above it and who also fixeth his mind is of course a twice born Brahmin.

271

Go and say, I have cast a great shame upon Vemana himself who named Vishnu and disgraced Siva and even Brahma. Let the one God alone be honoured.

272

Among them who are not wetted with rain and them who are not those who relying not on Vemana, follow not him (conduct themselves) wherever thou seek are not to be found. Never shall we see his equal.

273

Are there not eighty four lacs (84,00,000) of tribes of animals in all? As for the manner of their production in the earth, is he indeed that hath described it in your hearing, still to be called the mad Vemana.

274

He has thrown away his caste as water and slain his teachers (as Bheeshma in Bhārata) and nobly lied lies as big as elephants. Yet his name is just king--a great *Vepa* seed, bitter and worthless, 275

Locomotive animals all, till death, eat all excellent tasted things without leaving them, But immovable animals (hills and trees) are ever dropping their pride sorrowing remain.

276

You will say "We are versed in the knowledge of God" Ask yourselves--what is the meaning of Divinity? Tell, if you know whether he be whiteness, blackness or redness?

277

He knoweth not what sort of man he is, He knoweth not his former birth. For so debased a life why should be so careful? He knoweth not that this world is but an (*maya*) illusion of Ishwara!

278

He who wanders the various lands under the titles of the stranger, the recluse, of the noble Ganga of a hill or in the character of a man of exceeding beauty is yet one sole spirit of life.

279

Surely a teacher is requisite in the Siva creed and a teacher is evidently requisite in the Vishnu faith. What can the wretch of a debased nature learn without a teacher?

280

Surya lover of the lotus, was born in the race of Vishnu, husband of Lakshmi, the noble mother and as he duly goes his course, going about the lands and the earth; Vishnu nourisher of the elephant, travels as he does (for Surya is in reality but a form of Vishnu).

281

Let us know the source of the three Gods. First know one of the three, Then fitly with thy tongue offer praise.

282

The water in which the race of saints came plunging in defiled it. In which even Brahma being immersed cannot lift his head out of it. All men, whatever are plunged in this pond upto the middle.

283

By means of ambrosia all become stable. But if we seek ambrosia none can find it; ambrosia turns into venom--what a marvel this is!

284

Know well that this world is partly black, partly red, partly white (the three *gunas*--tamas, rajas, satwa). What is the reason that it should be all alike?

285

The ultimate has no lameness in his foot; He has no name in the dispute of his world. Understand that this is the bliss of others.

286

He was wonderfully born in the Brahmin class and being sunk in sin flowed thence into the other castes. Though born in the lotus, the sole of his foot is not wetted with the holy stream.

287

The king of hills (Himavat) is his father-in-law, the daughter of he hill (Parvathi) is his wife; a hill Kailas is his home; and gold hill, *meru*, his bow. Thus O Siva, thou art Lord of Hills. How art thou still given to such go between practices. (This is a sneer at sexual love originating in the creator).

288

The house is worldly connections, the bow is his weapon. The Five--lettered God is mother of redemption but all uniting with woman is but a lie.

289

If you twitch off a head of Brahma, they call it murdering Brahma. Brahma is a Vysya (a man of the third class), is he a Brahmin? If Brahma had even died would Siva become a Brahmin slayer. (This is an allusion to the base of the lingam representing Brahma).

290

Siva assumed the shape of the sharabha and slew Narasimha; which (masculine, *yēdi*) God is greater than Siva? Where is there one more worthy to be looked to?

291

Seeing that Vishnu abhorred not himself to be born in ten incarnations, to grow in them as to delight in them; if then thou do away the lustre of the noble married state shall thou hereby become one of the excellent.

292

Agajata (Paravati) causes him (Siva) who gave her half his body (see the mythology) to be slain (i.e., her worship as shacti, supersedes his)? If he cannot revenge this cruel is he man and not a woman?

293

The Veda is on every subject (words of the choultry). The signification of the Veda is a refuge (a branch of hold). Its rules are worthy to be known. Proclaim it consolingly in the world that the sound produced by closing the ears is subject to the state of meditation.

294

He who has seen the similarity of every generation and by wisdom knows the nature of the bathing, eating and lying in each, that man who thus knows how to walk is the *grihasta* (i.e., a perfectly virtuous man of the world).

295

If defilement attaches to food, it attaches also to the soul that thereby subsists. Food that is digested within us (let our soul) this is defilement. Food is the purification of the soul and the soul the purifier of the food. Thus united as the earth and sky are.

296

Daily does defilement flow down through the nine orifices, If this defilement of humanity be done away, man dies; foulness that never dies is produced in the loins.

297

Heedless of foulness and impurity, they eat three times a day, and worship him who sports within the soul (Brahma). He who thus attains the future life is the complete *yogee.*

298

That pious man who delights in bestowing house, garden, and field on Brahmins, long shall he rule the earth, and be filled with enjoyments.

299

The property given by a Brahmin to a Brahmin, though it be highly fruitful, yet cannot be enjoyed by a lord of earth (Brahmin). He must quit it.

* * *

300-399

300

As for the gifts of land bestowed on Brahmins, you may mention your having bestowed it. But if you tell others of your having made a Brahmin any other gift you shall lose the whole merit there of.

301

It is lawful to tell all men in the court that you have made a gift of land. But of any other gifts of your hand, you are never to tell others that you have given it.

302

Ignorant of the glory of the great being, all their external observances are like to a lion attempting to live on grass.

303

The fruit of your acts in a former birth though thou say--I do not choose it, it will not depart nor it will come for your saying, I wish for it, then resignation in the heart is best of all.

304

Having burnt up cupid with the flame of his eye he united himself in lust to (*Gowri*) Parvati. If thou look upon the might of this Siva even for a moment, thy sins shall pass away.

305

A woman dwells on the head of Siva and ever dues a woman dwell in the mouth of Brahma. Ir. the splendour of felicity does a woman dwell in tine noble breast of Vishnu. Thou alone Vema is able to put away women powerful as they be, 306

Our bodies are born unconsciously. Do not we bear them about, sunk in foulness. If we obtained an intellectual body how should we be continually reproduced in the world, O Vema.

307

Possess not thyself of wives nor sons. He that allows himself to suffer distress for these is a mad man like him who lifts a stone from the earth and places it on his head.

308

Through a sin committed ignorantly in a former birth, we are immersed in impurity and burdened with the body. But if thou be one of understanding how should thou be reproduced in the world. Thou shalt become immortal.

309

Sons are the barred doors of our earthly prison. Wealth and kin are the encircling wall and fools are the prisoners.

310

Unable to swim the stream of abstinence that lies across their path, the three gods are subdued with the hook (rope) in their noses by the bonds of marriage. Is not it then a joke for a man to say he will swim it?

311

If a creature kill a creature and give it to a creature, thus devoured, shall beatitude be attained by the slayers of animals?

312

Did not Rama cast the fire-dart, and dry up the sea, pass over, and return and stand still. Then did he not bring trees and hills and with them build the bridge?

313

Whatever thou may, thy life is not in thy possessions. Though thou possess nothing thou possessest life. The destiny written by Brahma in thy forehead is vile as the writing of a slut.

314

By not bestowing food on one who begged it off him in the former birth, he becomes necessitous in the iron age. His being now born wealthy is a testimony to the beneficent man.

315

The acts of the deeply deceitful man who plunders the *Bhutts* (adulators), poets, and others and feigns innocence shall very suddenly become the rugs that fall to a dog's portion.

316

A daring thief will plunder the property of poets and the fat of his sinews grows stout and strong, like a daring dog he roams to bite.

317

If thou fail to destroy the sins (lit, pains) that were committed in the former birth, how should they depart. Thy mind (buddhi) and thy acts being combined and untwined what can such men say to this? They must endure the fruits of their sins.

318

Be he a great sinner or a Brahmin slayer or merciless or base, when he dies if, he stay all his desires and meditate on Siva, he shall become (*muct*) happy.

319

Why shouldst thou muse on thy acts done in a former birth? They have become the life of thy present existence. If thou consider the acts, thy present life shall take effect hereafter. What understanding is that which cannot know this?

320

Urine turns into excellence. Birth is sure by its means. Being born it turns to gold and a man of excellence. All those unchangeable souls that believe in thee, thou shall make acceptable as the blessed above O Vemana.

321

The woman that cannot give meat or drink is deceitful. If then in a succeeding birth, if she wish for food shall she gain it? This is like longing for a vest?

322

They who in time of need sell for an inferior price; these are the men who in such circumstances hang even in diminished price. Why should they who accept it consent? Besides should they ever have agreed, still the act is not befitting (I doubt the meaning of this intricate stupidity).

323

If thou bound a *linga* on a *bhavi* and burn something that is *bhavi* and wear its ashes, shall one who is *bhavi* be unable to see Siva, because ye choose to exclude him.

324

If thou bestow the exalted *vaishnava* sect on one of debased caste and call him superior to Brahmins, this is like cleaning a toddy pot and filling it with the water of Ganges at Benares.

325

He who unasked bestows his property--this is the Brahmin Saint. He who gives only when asked is a mere giver But he who is poor as to beg again of him who has solicited his aid, is the Siva Saint.

326

What did Parasurama gain by slaying his mother at his father's advice? Was he not deprived of all shadows of refuge to stand by him and driven to *malayadri*?

327

There are abundance of those who recite the (*tantra*) treatises on religion. But there are none who mention the mantras. They have become powerless as the puppets of a show man.

328

Are not all those who revile Siva ashamed when they view the form *Dacshu*, the ram faced, and after seeing the precious dignity of adultery who would commit adultery?

329

What is the cause that being born in water and grown in water; he puts water away from him and uniting himself with women, he relies on this fleeting body.

330

The accomplished maid drinks palmwine and water and among the great she looses her petticoat and dances. When she has done her work, she puts on her rags again.

331

He that eats dogs (quells his passions) is the (*linga*) Janga Teacher. He that eats hog (quells his bodily lusts) is the Parama *yogee*. He that eats the elephant, how wise must he be!

332

On the fourth day of the moon's decrease, a girl brought forth. On the fifth day she dressed herself and seeing her vest as a screen she gave the breast to net babe (a mystic riddle not worth explaining).

333

In an alligator's eye an old woman brought forth; the chiefs of beings have not put away her uncleanness; if those beings come how shalt they put it away?

334

In a girl's hand is a bunch of desirable flowers. In that bunch four spouts (distillations); consider in them the soul resides.

335

At high noon (*mudras*) by the heat of the full moon (jyotees), the large bee (wisdom) rapidly fans the breeze (grow). By full faith the soul enters into thee.

336

He that knows his mother knows the deity. He that knows the earth knows heaven. He that knows heaven and earth vows himself.

337

There was a pleasing girl on a loft (story). The girl speaking--I conceived an intention. In that intention consider thou shalt see beatitude.

338

A tree grew on a bird. In that tree were thirteen seeds. Listen there is a tree in those seeds.

339

With a gurgling sound he swallowed down a woman. When he swallowed her the woman stared. He swallowed her down body and all. (Woman is delusion).

340

A woman adorned with (wearing) beauty. To wear them, plucks (roots) them out of the box; when she tries to do so, a chief widow arrested her.

341

The jewel of woman went to buy oil, bought and brought home the cut-oil. Can oil ever be cut? (worthless)

342

First there were three branches born in a tree. Spouts, boughs and leaves were therein produced. The flower, the bud (foot spout) and the full fruit fill the world.

343

With the widowed widow *maya*--they plunge and emerge in worldly pursuits. But when that affection has ceased, when her protection ceases those desires themselves exist not.

344

Born from thy mother, sucking thy mother's breast and playing roguish pranks with thy mother, what shall I say of the reality (tatwa) of the mother being in another transmigration--the wife?

345

If a masker openly and causelessly throw the hundred and first tribe into a well, shall he being a mere toddy pilferer attain a future life?

346

He who can turn fire into water and water into fire, who converts fire into wind, and if he himself be fire, he is the jewel of *yogees* (i.e., if by mortification he can purify himself from the impurer elements).

347

Its feet are ten and three tails, one head--Thus it openly appears roaming the noble earth ill at ease. He who can clearly understand this is *Ishwara* (a mystic riddle, quite worthless).

348

He lives well known to the people; but is not a king. He has a crown on him, but he is not Brahma. He knows and speaks of what is fit, yet is no *yogee*. Know who this is (pure fooling of *Para Brahma*).

349

It produces young ones in the earth and writes their characters on them, and suffer beheading. He is the chief of the Gods . He is lord of men. (Siva in his character of creator, fate and destroyer).

350

In a flourishing tree, a fruit was produced with three eyes, but is not Siva. It has a skin on it but is no *yogēe*. It has sweet juice. (mystic fooling of a coconut) 351

It dwells in light and shuts its eyes while it lays egg with delight. Surely the cuckoo practices penance on the bough.

352

Husband and son both (join) delight to touch and seize the wife's breasts. Such is nature in the world. If the son touched it, milk springs forth. If the husband touches it, 'that place' moistens with desire O Vema!

353

A whore devoid of lewdness is the devil's daughter; joyless work a plague of rubbing. Thus a village devoid of a liberal man is demon's town.

354

Say not, this one, she is not fresh and this one is fresh. Be she old or young, the enamoured paramour cannot quit her. Can you call an old buffalo's milk nasty? Love goes by liking alone.

355

The whore praises all the ways of the whoremonger. The whore's mother exposes his infamy. It is hurtful to meddle with a whore who hath a mother.

356

Without coition a woman becomes old. If it enjoys coition, the jewel of horses becomes decrepit. In the earth, the man becomes aged who with incessant desire indulges in excessive coition. This is true, O Vema.

357

It is ruin to go with a gypsy's whore who can restrain a sinful mind. If she will leave the village I begone elsewhere

358

A whore's elder sister will caress and kiss you. The paramour gazes at her through love of his whore. Those of the wife's side are all his relations.

359

Born in the *yoni*, ye long for the *yoni*; you grow by sucking the breast and still seize the breast. The soul devoid of shame thus perisheth in the world.

360

Among men who are born in the belly that contains urines by the churning which is the lowest and who can be marked as the eminent?

361

The leaf of which cupid has delighted to eat the golden lace that vishnu born from the lotus navel wears round his chest (Lakshmi), the little locket (box) which men ever delight to open and gaze into the hillock that is ever lovingly hidden, the cup from which Brahma daily drinks with thirst, the crystal vase that princes delight to light up, the fair diadem of Siva who seeks alms with a dish under his arm, the box of love powder with which even saints are charmed (or for which they long), it makes the mightiest sing and talk and dance like the fool and sports with them. Can there be any greater assembly of mischievous charms? (a beautiful and easy song) 362

He who serves the semen becomes the seed. He who serveth the holy streams becometh a God. He serves the excellent shall for ever be the deity. (This alludes to shactiyam) 363

Born by copulation and growing up thereby, he lives in coition (lit. becomes it). If thou canst lay aside the practice of this thou shalt attain the pair (Siva & Shacti).

364

He is prisoned in the womb, then gains birth and is wearied through the fluctuations of loss and increase through the Craft of delusion, how can he know either his origin or end) 365

When the day when her breast begin to bud she traps (*illegible--JBH*) with love. When they become hubbies she causes desire When her breasts dangle, spirits would not covet her.

366

When breasts are budding she is worth three millions; when her breasts are swelled, one million; when her breasts are flabby, she is not worth a farthing,

367

Woman is the mortar in which men pound to wear it out. But they weary themselves and begin to fall over her thighs throughout the world.

368

Him who loses his *langoti*, they deride as a monkey, drew him mad and hoot him off. Yet will not you loose your langoti in the very presence of your wife?

369

From the juice of food, the juice of the generative drop is produced. From the juice of the generatiyn, seed is formed. To discriminate between the juice and the seed is essential.

370

The forehead .of him whose fate is there written, is but small. The inscription in the forehead of the forehead eyed Siva and the common destinies of men are all easily erased by rubbing the forehead.

371

Infricans penom vulvoe, the zengam orders his affairs thus, so as to continue his race in the world.

372

He who has not learnt to reward him who bestows a girl, or a poem, comforts him not (cools his belly) nor enriches him...(incomplete)

373

No one will give away buttermilk as he will toddy; though they hoard up for the thief they will not bestow in virtue...(incomplete)

374

In urine are all bodies born. What matters your caste, and what is your intrinsic nature? He that ceases from envy and knoweth the abode where truth is placed, this is the noblest of men.

375

The hill over the womb and the slit in its centre are the long and short foot. Thus they seem mighty bands; enjoy sweet coition and be happy.

376

United with a suitable female, if one is stout, a stout boy will be produced. But if this man be powerless can the sons be strong?

377

If one's wife comes and consents and another's husband comes and shove it in. O how it hurts, cries the lady with her mouth; but he replies it is home (it holds).

378

The pest of the anus is known to the whole race; it cannot be loosed; the pest of the tongue is life (i.e., food causes life). The whole world is subject to these inconveniences of the tongue and anus.

379

When we behold the body of a woman we are agitated; but cannot perceive the nastiness in her belly. To what end is this body that lives in defilement.

380

Your wife was born from the (urine) of her mother and father and the son is produced from the (urine) of the wife and husband and yet what delight (a pun with) they feel in this (urine) life.

381

The smell of lust in a woman's body causes an emetic; let us not enter that leaky hovel. Surely there is little pleasure in joining thyself with thy wife.

382

Look on woman--when the period of life arrives she is menstruous; from time to time the menses regularly occur. Then what is the name of the woman and what has it to do with time.

383

It is sad feeling to praise the subvulvatees; and vile to praise him who has it over his head and ridiculous to praise him who carries it in his cheek.

884

Caste is a pariarism, a wife is a parcel of *mala mutra*. Can love be produced in the body towards such a wife? The mind through spiritual knowledge becomes a form of God.

385

Filth goes to the scourer and a block of wood falls to the share of the potters, fullness of the nails to the barber as is well known and as surely must the worshipper, attain the divinity to gain purity.

386

Foul defied cry they, ignorant of the source of that impurity. Defiled doth she retire to a corner. If she bathe in water the fourth day, do that impurity depart? Never shall it leave her.

387

Does not impurity flow from the nine orifices of the male? Do not they perceive it? How can a woman be so defiled as to be aside from men--surely all bodies are one.

388

There is no sweetness in the foulness of the loins. Yet there is some good in the secret parts. Will the defilement of impurity leave us merely by bathing?

389

In the earth on a mountain, in the pit on a hill, in the red earth in a white ant-hill, gold is produced. Surely is gold therein hidden.

390

If thou take the root *chedarasi* plant in its beauty, pour the juice of the moon plant there on and triturate it well, this shall produce a universally useful *anjanamn* (magic mixture applied to the eyes to show where things lie hid) .

391

If thou extract with vermilion the purest part of gold, and if thou form a crucible of potter's earth and if thou know not this science thou shalt reap no advantage from it.

392

This is a rock upon a hill. If thou closely combine him who is in the white-ant hill, so that the similarity shall be great. Then will gold be produced (spurious).

393

If thou put together a fruit with ripened husk and a grown *vepa* tree, and black sugar and touch them with quick silver, there will be produced gold excelling in value and beauty.

394

If thou take a stone and grind it on a stone knowing the nature of metal and unite them, if thou understand their union thou shalt thereby live.

395

One man chews and spits her out not caring for her. When he leaves her then a poor paramour wishes for his chewings; will not dogs lick the platter made of leaves which you eat of and throw away.

396

Though a fine wife's breasts be lovely let us think through the force of sin, on her breasts before now we have ourselves sucked comely breasts; let us not now think on breasts.

397

Of those we name teacher and pupil, which is last and which is first? If you desire to know and estimate them which is the greater, which is the less? Consider the teacher and pupil each as a teacher.

398

Seed is produced in the tree. The tree is produced in the seed, affection budding between them. Understand in the earth of the nature of the tree and the seed. For thus are the soul and the body connected.

399

The shame veiled in a word hides in the mind. The shame that is concealed by a petticoat is unfit to mention. But open shames are our seminal connections. Our shame is less as the cause is greater.

* * *

400-499

400

Reading, reading, reading still reading and still reading. Reading and reading, reading, some reading yet he cannot read so as to discern the great secret.

401

Who are those we everywhere term wife and husband. If thou will (take the trouble to) carefully view them, the truth is evident; but no one can see the joints of puppets (lit. skin images).

402

Take cow's butter and boil it well, mingle vegetables with it (branchless fruits). It is tasteless. The noblest of tastes is that of beatitude.

403

When we are born in the womb of our mother, at first, we had not clothing, nor shall have it at our latter end. Is not it then a joke for us to wear clothing in our intermediate life?

404

Like as a dog while hunting for bran that falls in with a heap of rice seizes it; thus does the wealth of the merchant fall to the lot of the hard and the cruel, 405

The *Vaishnavites* are saws in the assembly of kings (causing dissension). These are the chief gamblers of gamblers. They know not counsel but are swift in their eagerness for wealth.

406

The vile, leaves the man of worth and lauds the vile? Every man praises those who resemble him (asinus asinum fricat). Can a block give sense to a beam?

407

Why should a pearled tire (papita) be given to shaven widow instead of to a wife possessed of all charms? Why should a lame horse have a tasselled saddle.

408

Those men in the world who are faithful (*satya*) they shall also obtain wisdom worthily. When faith and wisdom are expired, a man becomes a

Brahmin, twice born. What hath he who has attained to do with learning. (The poet evidently had a double meaning, sneering at Brahmins.) 409

Taking fire in their hands yet scoffiing at God, the Brahmins have become debased; wandering in many diverse paths, all the Brahmins are ruined.

410

The leaf platters of Brahmins are the share of dogs of the street and the platters of pariahs alone are honoured. The platters thus honoured become the share of Brahmins.

411

A Brahmin will eat bone-food in which pounded skeleton is mingled. A married woman becomes a pēratālu. These give up their caste and character through excess of avarice.

412

What sort of caste is theirs who swallow the bearings of those demon--gods that devour palmwine and flesh. Thou with faith worship Siva they fail of becoming happiness.

413

Thou in the great destruction (the *pralaya*) all men were destroyed by the servants (pramatha) of Siva, yet have the Brahmins become enable to comprehend this.

414

The Vishnava sect is mere talk. There are no others more fallen than these wretches. Shall beatitude be attained by any sinner? (lit. by all hard men).

415

By birth a soodra--how can he become perfect (the best of the good)? The soodra state to a woman in every respect--his mother being a soodra how is he a Brahmin?

416

Whose son in this world is Brahma? If thou enquire whose son is Vishnu; if thou plainly enquire whose son is Siva? Men are ignorant of shame who dare call these persons gods.

417

The mother of the (setti) washerman caste washes menstrous garments, their father, great as he carries about grain. What is the pomp of these sons of asses?

418

Rambha, the celestial dancer seized the *Somayaji* (scorned him) and disgraced him, she covets with the somayaji, casting him down. Thus was it that this fellow gained the fruit of his sacrifices.

419

A man may get the title of dasari if merely has the fancy. He may be called jangam if he will give up a regular life. But he cannot be called Brahmin by any means.

420

You let your son eat off the same plate of whatever he be a son, you swallow his leavings--you cannot even see the least of true knowledge.

421

The *comatees* fall down at the gate of him that gives interest--he suffers the pains of hell. They will give you a penny or a farthing but nothing respectable.

422

Brahmins go on calling food and water defiled and throw them away ignorant of their nature. Food and drink are in truth Hari, Ha: a and Brahma indefilable by touch. They defile him alone who calls them defiled.

423

First by plunging in water Brahmin loses sight; by roaming he gains nothing but giddiness, by howling out the Vedas he turns into a dog.

424

If we take no food, the fire within the belly feeds on its own impurity. Then how shall he become pure who fasts and thus devours foulness.

425

One may wear a *longoti*, and wish to have himself a mini but cannot cease from the cupidity of his heart; the semblance indeed is one way and the heart otherwise.

426

He who seeing men dying and who knoweth the divine nature as removed equally from the death and birth, who thinketh deeply in his mind and gazette in abstraction he shall attain beatitude.

427

Like when a frog when beholdeth a snake that snake swalloweth the frog with great eagerness. Thus is the soul absorbed in worldly pursuits--who can extricate the frog? Vemana knoweth how to free it--are thou involved in worldly pursuits? This book shall release thee.

428

The verses of Vemana well considered admit of a thousand interpretations. If thou think on these, this shall produce refined wisdom in thee.

429

Let us look upon the fair assemblage of eighty four lakhs of animals as clearly the sons of Brahma; if thou attain wisdom thou hast the divinity.

430

The offspring of a multitude of all things and of all bodies and the five elements are born in this world. Those who fill their bellies with these cannot discern truth.

431

There being five joints (i.e., shoulders, thighs and neck) this car of the body goes about the world. If one joint be loosed that splendid car is ruined.

432

Quit the two weaknesses--hunger and thirst, the two of age and death, the two of pain and love, the two of pleasure and grief and the two of wisdom and ignorance. There is but one deity (in account) placed above the two mansions of the breast and forehead. Thus shall the gifted sage be happy gazing into his earthen vessel. (The signification of such riddles depends pp the fancy of the interpreter.) 433

He that knoweth the sunrising and knows the course of the sun and who knows the sunset in its beauty--He that thus knows the sun, he is a part of the divinity.

434

As long as the body lasts we must alternately sink and rise in contemplation regarding the *shacti* or creative power. When her protection leaves us we begin to wish for it not before.

435

Casting out from the ship the seven *dhatus,* five *pranas,* six passions, eight (5 bhootas and 3 gunas) and one delusion, the king mounts the vessel and goes about. This is tatwa.

436

Fairly establishing the house built on one pillar with its six stores, how shall one make himself lord of that mansion.

437

To be united with six passions, grief at the last; to be united with the seven becometh a cause of weeping. To slay in unison of these (for these to perish) is wisdom.

438

Relinquish the three affections, confuse the three, sink the three qualities, *gunas*, the three Gods and the three *shareerams*. The combination of the three, three and three form beatitude.

439

Believing the external world to be the divinity they scrutinise it. How should the external world (ed quod externumeast) of itself become divinity? Felicity exists in scrutinising that firmament within us that is the divinity.

440

Surely those are mad who, while there is one chief quality (satvika) in the three (*rajasa*, *tamasa* and *satvika*) leave it, unite the three, place them in their heart and unable to discern it are plunged in worldly pursuits.

441

Between the Ganga and the Yamuna (i.e., the two nostrils) there is a maid (spine) like a golden image, If thou unite thyself to her in love (i.e., meditation) without fail hereby shalt thou attain beatitude.

442

Few millions of goats died; only did one monkey mount on a leaf when ten millions of those monkeys died, a fox cried co, co--This riddle signifies.

Aja	a goat	Aja like wise means Brahma
Hari	a monkey,	Hari also means Vishnu
Siva	a fox,	Siva is Shiva who ultimately survives triumpth.

443

The tree of the back-bone is fixed on the fruit of its lower extremity and the wires of nerves are fixed. The fingers on those wires perform the (tripura tandava) dance of Siva in Tripura.

444

A cock touching sky and earth having horns protrude their points--splendour without a lamp shall shine.

445

At first it is a tree; at last it is not a bird; it has no mouth, but six fruits; it his not even one life and slays living creatures.

446

It hath no foot nor hand; but has a petticoat; no horn but rushes swiftly and bites at all men Without having practiced in a fencing school it slays us. This is a great marvel.

447

He that has an external throat with his mouth feeds on leaves; he has one leg and is all to match he shines and talks in the courts of kings.

448

When acquainted with the path of great construction of the body (acunchana) if at any time thou disregard the *moola bandhana* all the old men in the world shall become youths. (This mystic fooling signifies that what is apparently the meanest is of the first consequence) 449

If fixing thy understanding thou look and behold the light of the moon (i.e.. breast)...(incomplete).

450

Maya is not in fact the daughter in-law. She is the wife of all men in the world. Behold, she is gold, but such as cannot be plundered (nonsense, useful for words).

451

Brahma became a horse Siva (Bhava) became the saddle; *Adi* Vishnu became the stirrup. He that mounts on this stud is either female or male. I know not which.

452

The men subject to passions, on one side serpents (passions--*indriya*), crows on one side, the nine large tomcats (animal senses) on one side; the nine large paths, being restrained, the light (the soul) departed to the external, the tiger (ignorance), the fox (delusion) rose up and gazed; the dog (mind) perished--the men of the woods (apes) cried out, the soul has become Him, Him.

453

Meddle not with the (yoga) eight connections of the body, the six creeds or the three causes (*mantra*, *laya*, *hatha*). By the one remaining means (i.e., pure devotion) thou shalt attain happiness.

454

The spirit that is named without equal, having slain the being that formerly bore his name, and again caused him to return into life, Vemana can render his image (or brother) stable for ever. (Mystic raving) 455

What wonder is it that the tree of wisdom should grow with its root upwards (in heaven) and its point downwards (in earth); over its root is a lustful elephant (the eye) walking. What is the wonder of this? Like a distinguished soldier, an elephant (ignorance) swallow an ant (wisdom), what the secret of a marvellous tree (the Sushumna nādam) that never was born, being produced in the earth, on (the body) a rock and if the *chemanti* flower (chrysanthemum Indicum) the mudricas be produced, what is the secret of the birth? Behold if the all knowing and learned men speak distinctly, Vema listen to them.

456

In the earth a frog (the mind) seized five serpents (passions) and suddenly swallowed them. What is this? Two men of the woods (apes i.e., wisdom and ignorance) came and by themselves of themselves swallowed their young (their acts i.e., annihilated them), to a fox (delusion) in the Iron age *cāmadhenu* was born. In what way was this? Possessing intellect there was an infant that chewed; what was this marvel (wisdom absorbing ignorance). In seven modes of existence, (mahattu, ahankara, shabda, sparsha, roopa, rasa, gandham) mercilessly was might (delusion) produced and agitated men. What is this? The all knowing sages that have declared this, listen to them O Vema.

457

What is the mystery of a fly that screamed out and swallowed a bed? How was a mace produced in jasmine blossoms? Amazing, on a (marri)neem tree (ignorance) plantain fruits (wisdom) were produced; how was this? What is that dancing that the flower bodied woman knows. How did the five coloured parrots have power to swallow five mountains. Thus have the wise of old taught, listen O Vema.

458

He who comprehends the preceding three verses and can explain them truly he shall see Siva. What is there unknown to thee?

459

He who knows one, two, three and four, five, six, seven, eight, nine thus far, to the last what these are, that man is Vemana.

460

If they do not hesitate in 1006 ways water courses well turn as men turn. But a thousand ways are insufficient to teach the chief (root) wisdom to a piece of wood.

461

While impurities are perpetually flowing from the orifices of his body, how is it said that the recluse is thoroughly pure? O ye sheep who externally daub yourselves and fall into the hands of Fate!

462

In the eye flowing from moisture, in a boil flowing with matter, in a house the thatch of which is damaged, in a whirlwind, in the breast that the child sucks--how should there be any tightness?

463

If you say let us look behind, there is the well of (foulness) dirt. If you say let us look before, there is a nasty pit. Oh when they see a woman men fell down to pray her.

464

If fate (the female power) look at men they hide their faces. Unless ye eat the food of that Fate ye shall not be blest That power (fate) is the origin of the three Gods.

465

A girl is smart powder; but divinity is grain flour. The future state, in its excellence is fine *calama* flour. Can sages know the excellence of such flour.

466

If you say I will drink palm wine they abuse you violently; they abuse the entire body of him who drinks it. Yet he who drinks palm wine they entitle noble, for the recluse knows not the distinctions of good and evil.

467

The village of our body in which the deity dwells is Hill Town (the head); his is in back street (the spine). There in silence is the first house. We gaze and continually view it, this is the road of beatitude.

468

Quitting the bonds of the body he cannot go forth. Sargnee (Vishnu) walketh with delusion as, with his wife. If he, so mighty, is thus ensnared, what power had men to release themselves?

469

In Gandicōta there is a musk deer; it is not a great horseman. Be he great as he may be, that deer will mount (the hill) and overthrow him.

470

Pācanāti Reddee, and Mōtah Reddee and Tōta Pedda Yerra Reddee, these are all stubborn, wretches accomplished in all hardness. Thus have they gained celebrity.

471

Are all those creatures men who bear about sedan? He alone who enjoys himself within it is He (the God); shall the fruits of his good deeds be enjoyed by these base wretches?

472

The accomplished sages all meet and forming the mental figure, purified it with lime of steel--surely then lime is not the source of all purity.

473

He who eats lime (of stone or shells) possesses the philosopher's stone, chunam that exceeds in the touch of gold, is better to Brahma and the rest.

474

Lime is the best of all matters. Lime displays the present world in the earth and it also shows us heaven.

475

He who eats lime will be delivered from the ties of relationship which shall all be calcined; can it remain permanent? (lit. in the path) To Vishnu, Siva and Brahma never have any power over lime.

476

By eating it have the demigods and *munees* attained immortality. But they who see and scorn it derive then beauty from it. When men eat it they become demigods.

477

Is not the horse noble? Is not it all things? Cannot we attain Siva? If we meditate on him should we remain thus in darkness?

478

If a horse eat lime, it will grow great. How should it hereby attain and nourish the truth of desire. If a horse eat lime it shall become wise.

479

What is the purport of this world? Horse is the victorious steed. The horse is the highest of blessings. Horse signifies a pure substance.

480

There are seven living beings. The eighth (*maya*) is not living--all the mighty are in anxiety. If thou look into thy thought all words vary. (raving foolery).

481

If after mounting this creature, the horse, he cannot manage him, the *tatwa yogee* is in trouble. Let him mount the elephant of knowledge.

482

He who closely views the firmament being as a globe and duly observes the moon above it; he who views this well shall find it is for his good.

483

He who builds a house on the open plain (*bayalu*) and void of discernment wanders confused, is a wretch given up to his lusts. He who knows the (*bayalu*) open heaven is himself the divinity.

484

Maya, the wife laughing, the husband is weeping (the soul), the wife delights in adultery. That adultery pervades all nature.

485

A wife (*maya*) who hath no figure loves her husband, a man void of vanity is a stabbing hero, a man who is diseased becomes a soldier of God.

486

Whatever difficulties a man meets with in this world, it is not a place that can be instrumented to the attainment of the next world. Then they are not worthy however closely you view them.

487

How many are they that live on earth, in heaven, and between them has any one the power to count them; those who live are indeed those who die.

488

Though he can teach others and know for himself the instability of the body and the fleeting nature of wealth, he cannot yet attach himself to an adequate (illustrious) devotee and attain real perfection.

489

The sins that a wife commits, do with out fail fall on the husband. Of the good the husband does, half comes to the wife. Why is that we are not told that the sins of the husband also visit the wife.

490

Whether misers or givers there is not one in this world, who asks not of his friends; he that gives not to others, consider him as the chief of misers.

491

However many famines and sudden deaths, and terribly severe diseases occur, if long life be abundantly possessed by the tribes of creatures, why should they so perpetually sorrow and why at every word should they, being fools say I have nothing? Behold, the merciful chief spirit is alone our refuge.

492

A house full of holes and a worthless wife are alike. Like to a worthless wife is an idiot son; like an idiot son is a jeerer.

493

If God be ours (if the deity has been attained by us) even the destruction we shall rejoice in glorious majesty, he that knows not god shall remain a captive.

494

In vessel of water the sky is visible, but in the absence of water how can the firmament appear therein? Regularly (or daily) comprehend thou the splendour of god in the vessel of the meditating intellect.

495

He who makes his body to be as a mill, and his senses as the oxen, likewise converteth his acts into the oil seed. He through understanding shall like an oil-man with his soul his intellect shall as fine oil be freed from carnal impurities.

496

They who go on pilgrimages to sacred places travel league after league merely through forests, villages, lakes and rivers. This is the sum of their good works; whatever you wander (Vemadu) the divinity aideth and accompanieth you.

497

He who minutely views the soul in the body who showeth forth the body in the soul and who perceiveth the soul to be everywhere, he is become a part of the divinity, 498

What king is able to sustain and nourish the world composed (mingled) of earth and sky. How is it then that man assumes the name of (Lord of Earth) king?

499

The wisdom of a wise man is of continual duration but the fool possesseth no knowledge. To know the wisdom of wisdom, this is the end of knowledge (*tatwa*).

* * *

500-599

500

The earth is the noble mother; the seed is the father, the crops are sons, the produce of cattle (i.e., milk etc.), is heaven (because milk in various forms is offered in sacrifice), virtue is divinity. That is Truth.

501

The farmer begins by cutting hastily down the flower gardens of the god to build gates for the sluice (with the planks of the trees). Sinners are they who attempt such acts.

502

Sorrow shall follow and seize him who wastes grain. If he possesses grain his pain is over. In the veranda of the very whores of him who hath grain, men shall abjectly wait for gruel.

503

Bread and water are the origin of the glory even to the Gods. In this iron age it is the seat of all virtues. Food is as the elder brother of all men (a pun).

504

Food puts an end to difficulties; food alone is the dwelling of life, beyond all other things. Are there any in this earth who desire not food (instance of comparative?) If there be any, they must be none but Siva (*Ugrudu*).

505

If the beggar cries (Date obolum) he who replies 'Oho' how likely and asks him ridiculous questions, where shall such fools acquire honours? They shall perish roots and branch in their avarice.

506

What honour or what shame can the mouth full of spittle, receive a buffalo mouth, (mouth as gaping as that of a buffalo) is like a dry well. They cannot discern purity as they discern tastes.

507

However many curses (slaying words) we utter, they are but as wealth beheld in a dream, all fleeting, but a single blessing (word of life) suffices--it is unexhaustible as the mines of the Ocean.

508

He who after receiving the value the mortgage usurps, more than was settled shall lose that surplus and the original article alone shall be his.

509

Inordinate enjoyment occasions the loss of the original possession. Property put in pledge suffers a certain degree of loss. In the first case the original possessor sustains a loss.

510

If when the assembly has met, you give the full price, the cost will all be paid, but if instead of payment you give a bond with interest for it, it will occasion a heavy loss.

511

When a sale is made if a single farthing remains unpaid, a covetous desire may arise. If the property you have purchased come not into your possession without delay, you suffer loss.

512

If thou enjoy personal possession of the land and hold it for twenty years, this forms a strong title to it. Enjoyment constitutes the basis of written deeds.

513

If such a possessor holds undisturbed enjoyment of the land for twenty years--though the written deed exists or destroyed, enjoyment constitutes the strongest title to the possession.

514

In this world thou attain possession--the written documents form the strongest instrument of right. Consider enjoyment as the mother of the title deed.

515

In gift or sale you may dispose of what is your own. But cannot give to others that which belongs to your neighbour. If others give their countenance to such acts, yet how can it pass valid on the earth.

516

This man, void of all caste is the *yogee* worthy of honour. He is cautious as a cubbed tigress. The words of his rectitude shall never cease (very difficult).

517

(Pure sanskrit) By the possession of the four methods (gentleness, liberality, also the unison of discrimination, punishment) giving, secrecy, resolution, wealth and readiness--by these, the unparalleled man is king (very difficult).

518

He who nourishes the earth, who relieves dependants, who foresees what shall happen, who undertakes upright conduct, who surpasses mortality, who respects every creed--this man shall shine as royal saint.

519

Harischandra drawing near in truth, in former time, established himself in eternal fame. Truth is the chief grace of kings.

520

The class of half casts are seceders from the family ordinances, a wicked tribe; full of robbery and adultery. What more need we say of these cruel wretches that are heedless of right and wrong?

521

They mention not their own conduct but say *Dharmudu* (yama) is vainly given to anger. They listen not to a word in due season; but talk and chatter ultimately they shall fall into his burnings.

522

When a cataract (*pora*) covers his eyes, a man unable to see, tosses about (pora) begging that the cataract might be removed. But surely this is the unalterable punishment of his frauds in a former birth.

523

All men have one excellent dwelling. Beholding this house the heart is afraid when it is in dread; it (forgets the body) swoons when the body swoons; then are we resolved into the great spirit.

524

I will fitly teach all that dwell in the earth; that they may know the city (i.e., body) that beholds God is but one. Let not thy mind be corrupt and in it shalt thou gloriously behold Him 525

With this vile mouth defiled with spittle let us not read the *shastras* or *Veda*. Consider are they not thereby defiled.

526

The name teacher is very mighty; is not the most chief place attained through the Teacher. Teacher signifies light. To such a teacher let us remain attached.

527

Will not the word, 'I', equally suit thee? Surely if you lay aside of the fashion of saying thou and I, then shall He thou and thou I.

528

Let those who restrain all their thoughts and attach themselves to the deity, become even while householders, recluses and gain heaven. But if like the *budama* fruit they please all men, how shall they be blessed.

529

Him that truly know that God that dwells in the heart shall they call *yogee*; if thou know thyself thou art thyself the deity.

530

Water sinks into the earth; a sprout turns into earth (observe phrase); the plant is both husband and son to the earth-(This has occurred elsewhere). The earth is mother and wife of all men.

531

If thou give food to one who has failed (lost his opportunity), having failed (or lost luck) he will be ruined even by that food. When fortune is gone, food itself is death. (Simple construction, untranslatable in English).

532

If a poor wretch void of means and subsistence dies, no one who has means will go near him; will not men who have means go to those have subsistence.

533

Will not the life of the poor end? Will not they roam from place to place? They who will not look towards him who has no support, these are themselves destitute. (puns)

534

Wealth suits well the acts that we participate in it. Power is a tie on us. (The power is led on to great oppression). Wealth and power each do us harm. (loose version)

535

Shall those who while they have wealth labour and toil and in the feast days (on happy days) bestow on others what they ask, shall these be called hardmen?

536

Those who are not able to know the everlasting, and who are ignorant of wisdom who know not the truth, murderers, have no fate (course), but this, in the fire of hell and in paining hunger shall they...

537

Those ignorant souls that know not that this can be done (avuta) and this not (cāmi) ignorant of the truth, daily through impurity produce offspring; unable to know the spirit they continue to die and born anew in this world.

538

Bodies are transient, virtue is eternal, all the virtue we perform is alone the thing that cannot be ruined. These brutes of men though they see and hear cannot understand.

539

A village void of farmers is a sorrow to the *curnam*. The hatred of the *curnam* is a grief to the farmer. The farmer and the *curnam* are to each other like the buckets (pots) on a yoke.

540

If on any occasion the curnam scorns the farmers, their dwelling become unstable as a paper kite. If the *curnam* despises the farmer, the *curnam* surely becomes (upakaranam) a mere appendage.

541

If the *curnam* conducts himself as the farmers' desire, the *curnam* obtains good property and power. If he despises them, evil shall not fail of reaching him, the village being deserted.

542

All the attainments (learning) of a man in poverty turn to disgrace, even to him that is of celebrity and however great. Shame falls to the share of the base. (who repay it not) 543

Like as lotuses which if they leave the water fade; the rays of the sun who is the lover of the lotus affecting them; thus if thou leave thy due station it is certain that thy friends shall become thy foes.

544

How many lusts has the belly? For it men are in anxiety. For the sake of the belly, villages exist and so do forests. In someway or other provision is always found for the belly. Surely it governs men.

545

What shall become of the hard man who wishing to give gifts or charity says he will give it today or tomorrow and thus procrastinates? What shall become of his life? .He is ignorant of the force of delusion?

546

Our own kin (passions) are foes to us and our own virtues are our nearest relations. He who knows his own thought and that of his foe; this man is assured by Siva. (that is who thoroughly knows the good and evil propensities of his nature).

547

If we consider the conduct of men, surely no one is able to esteem it aright no more than we are able to esteem the purple hue of the *pindi* herb.

548

The villages (mahals) we possess shall not follow us in death, nor shall our jewels, our wife, children or friends accompany us. The alms we have bestowed shall alone follow us.

549

All the wealth of *Bāchanna* who was born in the Raya caste fell to the lot of the Bhatts (poets). But the wealth of the base was shared between his kin and the strange woman.

550

Manifest in the world was Guntupally Muttadu gifted with noble virtues. By means of bestowing food and through worship of God, was he absorbed in the Deity.

551

Behold the unrighteous who in the severest famine give the mere leavings of food to others; these shall be born again as dogs that lick defiled leaf-platters.

,552

Strange is that a man will embezzle the donations made either by himself or by others. It is like selling a wife and buy a slut instead. (A substitution of crime for virtue.) 553

The sinner that interferes with the charities established by himself or others, he shall for many years be repeatedly born in the earth as a worm and suffer misery,

554

Say not he is there or here. Vishnu dwells through all places shining in splendour. Behind him does the serpent follow the course of his *chacra*.

555

He has given some creatures feathers as a covering, tails to others, clothes to some, and leaves to others. Thus has God provided for all,

556

He who investigates in water the element (of fire) and ascertains it with delight in his mind--this man is like water of elemental nature. (awfully difficult)

557

A wife unapproved, who does not love you, a friend who desires you not, he hateth not these--he is a silly swain.

558

The state in which it is not disunited from the soul is agreeable to the body. But the state of separation is best for the soul. Therefore if thou obtain such a state thou shall enjoy its fruits.

559

Behold the world is bound with the seven cords of passions. Strange! with the sword of knowledge let us strive to sever them.

560

Let the fool first learn to know the Deity. (I propose reading అది నెఱగ లేని). He is himself unable to describe it. But when another dies he merely cavils like to a dog that can upset a pile of pots but is it able to erect it?

561

If thou eat a powdered bar of steel in medicine. it will make thee pure; if thou eat a bar of steel, disease will be removed. A bar of steel is thus superior to the tree of desire.

562

He who eats steel is the mightiest in the world. He who swallows steel shall dwell in the earth. What is superior to steel? nothing but the tree of desire.

563

Distress and sorrow are in proportion to our wealth. By sorrow is the body weakened; freedom from anxiety is the only possession secure from ruin.

564

He that loves the body undertakes to attain corporeal perfection. He who loves the body becomes a lover of God. When he becomes a lover of God, he shall attain immortality.

565

Those who know every distinction of soul shall never fall. These are not ensnared in affection for those who are later born. When water hath become a pearl, will it again be reduced to water.

566

Soon shall the sensual (*dēhi*) wretch who is blinded with attachment to his wealth, sons and wife reach utter ruin through his desires--alas! how shall this wretch attain emancipation?

567

First born in a bag of skin, if he be wise will learn what happened before his birth. If he cannot learn then he shall perish in his folly.

568

Through the deceit of the wicked and crafty thus Nay Harm are deceived and ruined. (Their raft is sunk--a proverb) Evil qualities and evil talkers are grief.

569

With these eyes how can we behold thee? The eyes that see thee are other and the vision diverse. Let us turn our eyes inwards and behold thee.

570

The wife that answers again to her husband is a bitch. The husband who persists in being coupled with her, these are like a pair of swine that tumble together into the mud, 571

A stumpy man is a sorrow and a spotted worm (serpent)is a grief, the longing for interest is a sorrow and the lions provider is a grief. A short leg or arm an equal plague.

572

Should a fire billet pride itself on being placed on another? To be on a tree, might indeed make it proud. Yet surely both the stick and the tree were created by the divinity.

573

Sinful gains are the cause of hanging the head--truth is surely the heart (ball of the soul), but to know this requires firm wisdom.

574

When a crane sees the moon it cries 'Co' and mounts on the summit of the banyan branch on the hill. The fair coloured moon is placed on the head of Siva.

575

If thou art beaten, reviled and bound fast, and with all violence, it shall not go well with thee (tiradu), unless thou refrain from saying thou art cruel, and meditate with firm mind on Siva.

576

The waters of the firmament doth he hold as a bunch of flowers in his hand in noble beauty. He that hath such surpassing power is the teacher of teachers.

577

Woman is like a box containing a young serpent; if thou put anything in this box and after closing it, thou try to pull it again she springs out as a great serpent.

578

They talk of what they call shame? Where doth it reside? They talk of hunger. Where does it lie? Where they are I suppose.

579

When man accepts alms and when he possesses fortune, he is a fool; he suffers anxiety in his mind for the body he inhabits.

580

Happiness shall never flourish with him who gives not meal nor drink. He shall be as a widower. Besides, shall the deity dwell with him.

581

If thou fasten a stone to a gourd with a rope it will grow elegantly without a curve. But were you to fasten it to a dog's tail, would it become straight?

582

What are we to think of the slaughters of these cruel half cast wretches (born out of the limits of the caste) who being themselves rationed slay animals without any offence and guilty and eat them.

583

If you with displeasure take a meal in the house of a person you dislike then one thing happens or you gain your end. It is as though you got it not evidently to both parties; that food produces hatred.

584

Like water on a lotus leaf (which rolls of and leaves it dry) walked Vemana. seeking God. O trust not to this illusion. To this mind, the lord is incomprehensible.

585

O Vemana! thy powers are not yet known even in the least. O Vemana! let us know how great it is thy pleasure to be hereafter styled. That is, thou alone art all we have; who else is our refuge? (admirable, simple)

586

Vemana is like to a man without food, void of anger, in every place at every (word i.e.,) moment, also in the form of verse has he spoken decidedly and so that it might be understood by all, in the earth he assumed the form of Siva, who is there who, time after time, is equal to Vemana?

587

What does a foul feeder care for excellent food? What does this body care for the light of wisdom? Know this and hereby learn the Vedanta.

588

If, viewing the *yugas* of the world as we pass through our transmigrations, we be not entangled there in, but in each yuga we become penitents, suffering sorrow and distress, the brilliant glory shall dwell in our soul.

589

Hearing he heareth not, being mad seeing he seeth not, this is *yogee.* He receives homage from the noblest of men.

590

Look on all pleasure. Surely it is sorrow. Our sins are the parents of even our virtues. This is as though a robber should wish to be impaled. The punishment will befall him unsought.

591

If you have hold of the root of a tree why go search all over it? If you possess the philosopher stone why (grieve) take further trouble regarding the voices of birds that knew where it lies or regarding the caves of the hills where it is?

592

If thou think on thy wife and children with great love, if thy desires be attached to thy wealth, surely there is no salvation in the world for this man.

593

Like as a cuckoo enters the nest of a crow, like as a maggot lives sustained by a wasp, such is the ruined teacher, (what sort of teacher) that knows not the truth and salvation.

594

How bright is the eye of the lover? It ever gazes on woman. Where is there anything like this? if thou look on the image in the eye how small it is?

595

They will not give to the poor as they will to the chief in the earth. To a (Brahmachari) student they will not give as they do to a woman. They will not give for wise what they will for wine (lit. toddy).

596

They are pleased when they see a village thinking it will be good residence; when they see the wilderness they are alarmed. He who looks upon forest and town as on; this is the settled and pure saint.

597

He who lauds the base, and roams and rambles in mendicity gaineth but fatigue. But be is superior who guards the brute senses (lit. sense--cattle) and shall shine both in this world and the next.

598

God causes us to possess the skill of composing verse. With apt skill and correctness, Vemana having duly performed (sandhya) draughts, (nishtha) meditation, (homa) oblation, and offering of water (tarpana) to the manes has had the happiness to compose it.

599

He who desires not any enjoyment, who ceases from loving and dislike, and who looks for the attainment, soon, of beatitude, this is the king of yogees.

* * *

600-699

600

The grief of a poor man becomes a great demon, an unuttered (invisible) trouble cannot be spoken (seen); But the anxieties of a rich man are still greater. What can there be beyond this?

601

The writing written by the hand perishes (spoil) not though thou blot it out (spoil it). What is written by fate cannot be done away even with water. The writing of fate in the forehead will not be gone though thou rub it with sorrow.

602

How should this animal life become assimilated with God? Shall we compare a village cur with a sage (or saint, yogee).

603

To the liberal man, the vessels of the mundane egg will fall into his hand. The demigods will become his dependants. Liberality becomes the residence of all modes of knowledge. Through liberality no grief can befall us in the world.

604

Behold, if thou say not, if thou refuse not, if thou oppose not, if thou dislike it not, if thou say it is not thine, that which is thus given is liberality.

605

If thou reproach others (abhor), if thou esteem not strangers as thy relations, ignorant of what of what is right and wrong and lay not hold of heaven (phrase, be puffed up). the liberality thus bestowed is no liberality--it is hoarding up.

606

Those who grind (i.e.; plough) for the good of others, those also that are dependants on princes--these are the men who are like milk and payer of taxes; the farmers are ignorant of language.

607

Though they be greatest of misers and hard and thou full of mischief, an evil doer when he boils over a cupful must be skimmed off. But they should not be called causers of the death of others. (That is, pride should be checked just enough to render it harmless.) 608

A degraded caste is a caste that has set aside all distinctions; the tribe sustains all creatures. Those who are of such a caste both here and in the next world are the Universal prop. (the farmer tribe) 609

The endless cupidity of merchant, the fruitless showers on the rocks, the interminate search made in the sea, the insurpassable light of the moon and to these there is no end. There is no path (to heaven) to the man of impure speech.

610

The sin committed by a people shall fall on their prince; about half of the good done by the prince shall come to the people. How then is it that the sins of the prince fall not on the people?

611

Would thou you were to look on a cow with affection like the affection with which you view a woman. The man is so much drawn by merit as by pleasure. What can we think of the conduct of a sinner.

612

All the excommunication of a Brahmin departs by the (*amrita*) products of the cow (panchagavyam). The faults of a servant are removed only by punishment. The impurity (menstrual) of the *Lingayath* is all removed by mere smearing with ashes.

613

A dog knows its own mind, pleased with it. But a man knows not it his own wishes or nature nor can see them in this iron age.

614

The frauds (lies) of a woman are impenetrable as a wall. A man's fraud is but a grass screen (tatty). The arts of women are ceaseless as the voice of a cricket.

615

He who holds as his own the afflictions that befall others is the man who shall remain and live in the earth. He who knows the next world well is the greatest of the noble in this earth.

616

The stony hearted wretch though be cut his body to pieces, yet will not give a penny; if you wish for a cow at his hands can you get it? It is vain as longing for gold buried under a hill.

617

The born villain, who through friendship (covetousness) that originates in wealth; knows neither himself nor his neighbour, not seeing out of his eyes with all pride; to go and beg of such a fool is all hard indeed.

618

So hard a wretch becomes the possession of the flame. The life (man) void of kindness shall waste away in water; the soul full of cruelty shall be the portion of cruel plunderers.

619

He who the worthless wretch who after daily exciting at hopes last says I cannot give it, his life is like to a radish. At last he loses all power and waits for the favour of others.

620

They who compare the breasts of an young woman to balls of flowers--the worthless wretches who are captivated in this earth. There is a lump of flesh there--what else is there?

621

He who lives after losing his character be he who he may, can he have any distinction? What dog will not lick a dirty dish (spittle leaf)?

622

Fools cry for food, food, If they cannot get wealth. Can they procure food? How should you fail of food if you have wealth--however many scarcities should occur.

623

When a man has lost his refuge let him not draw near to one in poverty. But he should go to him, he will turn him into a mere straw (with which platters are served) or into ashes.

624

One cannot give his sorrow to another; nor one can share his happiness with another. Those who feel either sorrow or good cannot know its intrinsic qualities (lit. semblance). Surely time (Pluto) shall know their true nature.

625

Hitherto ignorant to a miracle of what he himself is doing, born as a man yet unknowing both evil and good, he has sunk down to predication,

626

Like as honey is produced in a hillock (or ant-hill), like as a ruby is produced on hill, like as fire is produced in a stick--thus produced in the earth; let a man bestow on others.

627

Of what use is the man who when the wearied guest asks food compounds not for him, the nine condiments with salt, to quench his exhaustion. The disappointed guest remains unfilled.

628

They call the crow the most degraded of birds. None perceiveth the excellence of the crow in the earth. Man gives food to the crows and worships their feet. (This alludes to a practice of commencing a meal by giving a morsel to the crows.) 629

They say that the crow is the most degraded of birds. At the time of marriages they will not let the crow approach. Then why do you place food before it and salute it?

630

Like a boy looking at his shadow, who looking at his shadow forgetting himself, so are those deluded creatures who looking on their shadow call themselves kings. What shall we think of such fools?

631

The stone hearted hunter, who severs the mothers and the young of creatures that have heads (fruits are considered as animals void of heads)--when this hunter dies in the earth, when he falls on the ground, he shall be, of no use even to vultures.

632

Were not they born as ourselves in the earth? Have they not a life like ours? Oh! what an act is it to slay an anima! that has instinct (or reason, jyana).

633

The great whole continues in one mind. Their madness alone prevents men from knowing this. If thou walk in the knowledge of him that is our abode--it is enough.

634

Unknowing the path of thy future life (transmigrations) and if thou consider all thy enjoyments as permanent thou shall be separated like a fish from the water. In the end none but this shall be thy fate; thou shalt melt and perish.

635

He who though reviled or struck answers not again who looks neither this way nor that nor starts nor will consider himself the person in question nor is any way agitated--such a man becomes the Divinity.

636

Learn to know that great agent of all acts, O! Vema who wieldeth the thunder bolt, cleareth it from impurity and with its ultimate essence (i.e.. nectar, pure water) now fishes the iron age 637

The attachment between the teacher and the learner is very deceitful, Why should we explain or shew it. With subdued longing after beatitude if ye have full faith, thou shalt attain it and not otherwise.

638

When snakes are performing coition, you may catch them cleverly (unrivalled) and in a wonderful manner. But you cannot get the obstinate together and seize them with a prepared heart.

638

Consider fully the strength of thy shoulder and dispute not with the wile. Is not a stone broken by a pot of milk? (Boiled milk is set to cool on stone stands which thereby are split).

640

Where in the earth is the place where he is not beheld? He exists in everything. Who am I; who is he that I am not--know this truth, O Vema.

641

He who bestows either his own property or that of others shall become rich. Then let him think why he should entertain the smallest fear; ultimately heaven shall be his.

642

If he does good to others and gives the property of one to another (res alienas alieno si det) he shall inherit heaven. Is wealth anything in comparison with heaven?

643

What is the nourishment of others to the wicked? The sinner transgresses the lines both of regularity and affinity. What does obstinate know of the clues of tenderness, what distinction can such a one attain in this earth?

644

In those who prosper in their undertakings may distinguish themselves with a waste of words in any matter, but in a time when you are not in favour, no one work will prosper with you, however large your possessions be.

645

Be he an out caste or of any tribe whatever, he cannot rid himself of poverty. Will the poor man be disgusted at leaving?

646

The man of prudence who has bestowed the gift of land on Brahmins (observe scansion) and his heart on his dependents and who has (given half to) slighted the worthless, how brave is he?

647

The man that understanding all wisdom commits of his wealth, one share to the earth, one to others and one to the poor who thus shines, he, when he dies shall dwell in heaven.

648

The woman who holds her husband's words as the chief good and who loves her lord with affection shall by burning her body fully inherit heaven.

649

Those senseless corpses who give alms to the re-born who have separated themselves from dung and urine, these shall be produced again weeping and in sin nor released from transmigration. (Spurious) 650

He who after having been imprisoned in the ties of oxen, wealth, women and sons, is the agent in releasing himself, there from, can his glory on his virtue be comprehended even by (Sridhara) Vishnu? (Spurious) 651

These sinful men who having it in their power to give up the restraints of their children, women, cattle will not yet cast off these ties, these are void of shame and of manhood. (Spurious) 652

The whole race of man is in possession of twelve fruits. (that is, men receive in the next birth twelve percent on the sums they bestow in alms). But whatever they bestow on Brahmins shall return to them with thirty six percent. (evidently apocryphal) 653

He who when the land he had bestowed is lost, bestows other land instead on the original tenant, thus shall form a great blessing to the agent in such an act.

654

If the possessor loses his possession, this is no fault of the bestower. If the holder enjoys the gift, the giver hence derives stability.

655

He who usurps from the Gods, the Brahmin, the poet or the adulator, the gift bestowed either by himself or others, and grieve them, this man shall live till he devour dung without measure. (evidently apocryphal) 656

To devour a mortgage or the fruits of such a possession is a great sin though the committer be a king. The tenant alone has the right to the usufruct, to the exclusion of the land lord.

657

He who mortgages, suffers a certain loss, he loses part of his living. The acceptor of the pledge derives satisfaction therefrom. But he is ruined if he begins to covet it.

658

They who recognize (pity not) the nature of the irrational (uneducated) animals and contrive how to take mortgages from them, these are themselves the most brutish in the earth.

659

The thing that is nourished with *vasa* herb is poisoned by the *vasa-nabhi*, which also secures the body from *venom*; if thou comprehend this thou shalt become him who knows the secrets of the heart.

660

Ignorant of the chief good, void of sense, he sinks in darkness. That saint who is perfect shall know all the great secret.

661

He is a fool who gives his hand to another in assurance of security while he himself is transient as a figure in a mirror; void of happiness why should we contract marriage in this fleeting life?

662

What wisdom can he have who knoweth not knowledge? The fool never shall know God. What is the chief God (tatwa) to know the wisdom that is within wisdom?

663

Dwelling in the false earth, unable to reach heaven, grieving in their members, enduring sever penance-never shall these see happiness (tatwa).

664

A man of the sea may go to sleep with another. Know that an entire creation exists in the vast deep.

685

This world being continued by means of birth, death and sleep--a man's calling himself (observe grammar) a jangam therein, is not understood by any of the ignorant men of the earth. (i.e., ignorant recognize not holiness) 666

Water is changed into the body and the body into water and into immutable matter. This does the entire world of being exist in water.

687

If even a boil rise on the back of a man of virtue, it will become notorious. But if even a marriage happen in the house of a poor man, no one hears of it.,

668

What you call the Goddess of the earth is mere clay. How many fair beings are born from the earth that Goddess alone knows, but no man knows the origin.

669

They, heap up earth and wallow in mud but they adhere not to the earth but turn again, and are mingled with earth. Where shall they then depart to?

670

The scamp who cannot give up connection with a *Viti* woman (of the sword-playing caste) will carry about her mat and hovel (or tent) till death. Never care or aspire to an intimacy with the *Bhagavat* (actors who are respectable).

671

When they behold their refuge Vishnu or wealth, or studies that have pleasing taste however great they be, all men feel desire.

672

A man who is sent (lit. who sent) into the world, hear me, consider not one thing eternal and another temporal; such is his conduct. His projects constitute his family; and the destruction of his projects shall form the ultimate bliss.

673

The words of truth are equal in excellence with the streams in which Siva is; (*abhisheca*) bathed. The body is his temple. He who hath attained peace and placed with God in his soul, this is the Siva Yogi.

674

No numbers of corporal bodies form an obstacle to a death. To what end is that knowledge that teaches not how to avoid death; this is mere thievish fraud. Shall salvation be hereby attained?

675

Whatever shape we behold, it shows thy form. To view thy form increases wisdom; if understanding increase, a man is held to be the lord.

676

Carnudu was noble; who in the world is greater? He meditated bestowing gifts, no man knows of the excellence of him who doth no good to others.

677

Ignorant of the stability of wisdom the variable mortal roams the world. The ignorant wretch cannot consider why it is he thus roams.

678

When a man does not know what to do with his time, he cannot get on without listening to some learning or other. But this is fruitless; famina not audit murmura cassor inter futuendum?

679

To what end do the men of the earth practise austerity and meditation? There but one mode to behold God. Let not thy mind wander and thou shalt know him.

680

What has palm toddy to do with gentle behaviour; why all this care about appearances that are merely with a view to gaining bread? To what end is this body, which is destined to the earth of the cemetery.

681

If you powder nitre and tulasi (buds) together, amalgamate then upon gold; mix the milk of the dushta plant and mingle these upon a plate of copper which will thus become gold.

682

If thou pour milk in and boil it the tin will shine. If thou observe the proper moment and take it off the fire, it will turn to silver. This is no lie but the truth, Iswara.

683

If thou take a certain medicine thou shalt be able to rise from the earth; if thou take a certain mixture thou shalt be glorious. There is also a drug that quelleth fever.

684

Cattle that fall down in the staggers if they are fired and thus come to life again. Shall the milk of fired buffalo be held vile.

685

If he receive great wealth, he forbears to take it; he reviles the respectable and drives them off till they fly. Will a cow of degraded blood acknowledge the noble?

686

Numerous as creeds be they are not permanent in the earth. Truth is but one in the earth. It consists in leaving every creed and beholding the very deity.

687

In the real composition (lit. rising) of a cloud within the cloud there is thunder and thunderbolts in abundance. Then to understand what "cloud" implies and the might embodied in it is great task (revise).

688

If a seed be damaged, it cannot grow; if the seed be not injured, it grows. Then surely the seed alone is Viswakarma, the creator.

689

Though you hear of him, be not thou ever united to him, If thou see and unite with him, your desires will unite in affection. If from merely hearing of him thou be united to him, your love will depart. Such is love that originates in hearsay and sight.

690

The humility of a mad man is great. The widow when ruined veils herself, and the son of a prostitute performs the rites very duly.

691

He is a mental wax cloth (changeless) and a cave formed by bowed banyan trees. This farmer Vemana took all men and taught them well; thus did he gain renown.

692

A guana will live a century, a serpent will creep for ten centuries, and the crane will live in a pond for a thousand years. He who possesses man's chief good (wisdom) is the only excellent one.

693

If they say he knows not, surely he had no knowledge previously. If he begins to say I know, he knows the root. Let the mouth of him who says I know, when he knows not, be filled with a basket of ashes.

694

(Observe comparative) The dog has somewhat a better quality than man; for if we consider man in the world he is worse than a dog, if he be void of excellence.

695

A shop keeper's devotion well, never turn to any use. Through a covetous disposition he sinks downwards. It is as agreeable as tiger entertaining a saint.

696

A dome, ponds all about, cars and herb gardens, temples---all these arc very fair. But if you go to serve the God, all these divert the mind.

697

Until married, they are in subjection. When the cord (about the throat) is bound, they look scornfully. To be in subjection under woman is a thing not to be spoken of.

698

While the ears, skin and bright eyes, the tongue and nose continue, the soul remains; the spirit thus dwelling firmly in the body shines as the chief thing in the world.

699

What our own history will be and what those of our connections will be, if we wish to hear or see this futurity, the Gods themselves know it not.

* * *

700-799

700

Consider that thy mother and father are thy first instructors; Parvati and Siva are the greatest of teachers. It is a shame to call those teachers who are hired.

701

Whatever orpiment may be, there is not the least tin in it, though the three (powder, tin and lead) be found, it is not attached to them; but in the flaming fire is tin produced.

702

He smiles, he reads, he sings, whatever he do he is not pained, but pleased with all and at one time will forget all. He is young, he becomes old. Consider who this is.

703

If the water exudes and stands, mud is produced; but when thick rain pours, it will not remain. Reveal not this path but know it well (thus does sloth reduce men to sensuality).

704

The water shows the might of a ship; the plain shows the power of a car; but the power of a woman is seen wherever she be.

705

Who am I to think in any mind or who am I to be without meditation; alas the deity appears to man, and conceals itself.

706

The great family being thus extensive, is it a wise practice to think so much of the tribes of the various rishis? Can a monkey of the woods govern the world?

707

He who desires not milk, water, ghee, boiled rice, women--this is steadfast soul. He shall not fail in a single point nor walk in another path.

708

The swan knows water from milk, but how should the peacock know it. Then can a brute beast know God?

709

He will bestow on the vile and the jesters; he will give it for a *pariar*, skin, the son of a *pariar*; or to the drab of a fair, he bestows not on the excellent.

710

They know merely the teaching of the ancients, they have not the smallest sense; they gain nothing but wrangling; sad work like a thief who has no pleasure in moon light.

711

They talk as if life were eternal and pride themselves greatly, the fools. All beings are as sheep bound for sacrifice before Yama.

712

The divines call divinity; if thou consider well, it is with thee already; but they cannot see the form that is before them.

713

In their mind they cannot discern the form of God. Those who can view it in their mind exist not in the earth; but he who searcheth in his body and recognizeth it with delight in him, is the noblest of *yogees*.

714

The mind is the fire that produces both good and evil; surely then let us know its greatness and its meanness in the closing and opening of an eye; does the mind roam afar is not this evident?

715

Born from coition were all men and thus they long for it; without hindrance all haste to that by which they were produced.

716

If life have passed away for even half an hour, hath even Brahma himself power to vivify him? Hath Brahma then power either to slay or cause to live?

717

These words of discrimination, thus spoken by Vemadu. This insane conduct of Vema proves to be adverse to all fools. But to the wise, they are felicity.

718

Knowing that this book is a means of attaining both this and that world, they who write. read, hear this, it shall slay by its might the acts they have hitherto or (during life) done, it is even for others the path to beatitude.

719

This is not such learning as are the *Vedas*. This is not the language of a hero (such as the Ramayana). This is no painful knowledge. It is no great thing. This is that sweet knowledge that stays the mind. That is fragrant which is soon learnt (for svādu some read sādhu, here and in the next verse).

720

He who goes on saying I will give to you; but whenever you come to him puts off the time; the slaves that merely make false promises be they hanged in a noose.

721

The verses of Vemana may be interpreted in a thousand ways if thou closely consider them. By reading and again reading then thou shalt attain curious wisdom.

722

All those excellent ones who have read with sound sense a verse uttered by Vemana, these shall be exalted to dwell on the head of Siva (Somu); let then with thorough consent study them with wisdom.

723

To consider omens and all circumstances with interest, regarding a marriage with the daughter of a maternal uncle--It is all one sea that you enter.

724

If both parties are in poverty, let them by as much money as seems requisite, prepare a vessel of rice, and give the bride. Eat not the bread of prostitute.

725

What thou it be son-in-law or no connection, we have set forth the proper rules; not even a leaf trembles unknown to god.

726

Though thou are poor, if thou say to a man, I will give thee my daughter, ask not for gold with harshness; to accept gold from him is vile as if you were to take your own daughter.

727

The boundary of the village appears to no one (yēriki for evariki); it is earth not again apparent void of mark, it cannot again be found; consumption (or tenanting it) is the only sure boundary which does not depend upon stones.

728

The kings and princes who trusted the boundary stones have left their food, fallen and perished in the earth. The sons of demons who destroy these stones retain their villages and estates, and live there. (This is evidently aired at the Mahommedan government--estate is here mahal, the Persian word).

729

That possession that we have held for three generations without paying a sean as homage, the usufruct we enjoy is our strength. No other means, however numerous, are of any avail.

730

The writing, the possession and the evidence--in these three rests secure enjoyment of long duration; even in the courts of heaven they say these three have great weight (easy, pure sanscrit).

731

If the objections be good that disturb your ancient enjoyment of property, the writings are the basis of all, and set aside the old tenant, if his right be not good.

732

You may speak a hundred words but beware of writing down one. No evidence is required if the writing is produced. But in case writing is wanted then indeed good witnesses are required. (easy, pure Telugu), 733

When both the writing and enjoyment are combined, then is the evidence sure. When the writing and enjoyment are both wanting all other evidence is fruitless.

734

If along with the first witness an opposing witness be adduced, the preceding witness is of avail. The latter witness is the source of in influence. (lit. power.) 735

No authority (lit. great men) will accept of a (metca) sole witness, though he speak. no one will lend him an ear. If Item be two witnesses we may hold it true. A respectable house holder is the only witness.

736

When a great combat for a boundary begins, rather than killing each other in the dispute let old farmers who know the origin walk the path of the boundary. (Disputed boundaries are thus settled by an experienced farmer being appointed to walk on the correct line of path demarcation).

737

If one regard not right and wrong, and in any degree void of foresight, change the boundary path, desiring the worthless stones, and have them removed, and put his foot there (to establish another path), sin attaches to him.

738

It is fit to put diverse marks off the fixed boundary stones, foreseeing evil. Walk with a view to the present and the coming world. The next world is known to thee O Vema!

739

If you perform the ceremonies of donation (by pouring water into the hand), and provide copper tablets, connect them with a thick ring and on the joining of the ring the royal seal be affixed, this forms a sasanam (charter) in the earth.

740

At an (hour when all the people of the village come along with him, with appropriate observances with a drawn sword, let him walk separately and lay down the land mark with care.

741

Behind the man while he is digging the boundary, let the opposite dig an opposite bound and let all the chief men give him their blessings.

742

Let a farmer who is void of even the least deceit quickly and without timidity walk on the track of his feet, and let the good and chief men who know the fact also walk it.

743

The (jewel of calculators) good accountant who takes a pole thirty two feet long, places it and measures it; let him receive the blessings of the people and live in virtue.

744

The writing of the excellent man who measures the land leaving on each side of the measuring pole six steps as long as a cow's foot steps (unapportioned to either), that writing will be stable and able to reply even to the writing of fate.

745

Those men who cause the land to be measured (colva cheyu) with arithmetical standard of the pole and the rod and with skill know to supportion the compensation of the foot (measure of a bow's foot allowed on each side as verse 744). These are arithmeticians.

746

The use of having eyes is that he may know the quality of the field and the fitness of the tenant. If when he measureth, he regard not the rules of calculation, but does it hastily in the space of a twinkling of the eye, he shall depart void of male offspring.

747

He who knows the due shares of the crop and the fruitfulness of the lands, well versed in equity, suitable council (lit. contrivance), who knows the due division of shares pertaining to the government and the farmer, and on his guard against sin (injustice), he who knows also how to write all his is the chief (lit. jewel) of men.

748

The measurements of tanks and ponds, the measurement used in fields and small plots the measurement along boundaries without hindrance--to know the rules for these is a victory.

749

All those debased ones, who not recognising equity, measure the earth with a pole and over-reach in the measurement--these shall in the transmigration be born as leeches (the irregular floundering pace of which resembles their careless measurement.) 750

Parched fields, dry without rain, if excessive rain fall, are destroyed. He who looks to his crop expecting crop upon crop, a luckless wretch is he wherever he be.

751

They who are distinguished (or humble) in instruction, in recluseness, (not exact means) and devotion, and those who are no evil doers (mischievous) but united to wisdom--the verses that Vemana has nobly written are numerous by the number of thousands, beyond the power even of these men to write. (a singularly complicate verse).

752

A woman who gives no food or drink is no true wife to her husband. She is rather his destiny. The husband who is united with such a woman perishes without the chance of being born again. He will perish degraded and become a reptile.

753

Composed of desire and cupidity, and of stubborn hearts are women. What can we say of the conduct of women? Faithfulness is their chief virtue. They are in other respects mere figs--fair without but worms within.

754

Women perform (pettu) sraddha (funeral rites) to women; what witness is there in women to do this. Then performing (iduta) it to women, better it performed to stones!

755

By the anniversary ceremonies the whole caste is ruined; by the conduct of women all respectability (shame) is destroyed; by ponds that are spoiled this world is; destroyed (good water being thus wasted) and life is ruined by slanders.

756

When a woman is called to attend a funeral, the funeral is a (useless) ruined funeral. Males alone can be the performers or guests herein (carta, bhocta).

757

To the funeral feasts of widows, why instead of inviting widows, why do they invite Brahmins; to the funeral of a married woman ye invite married wives.

758

If thou give the funeral feast to widows, void of means, they would rejoice, in every one of thy acts; but through thy neglecting this, thy former acts in a preceding birth become hateful in this world of earth, sky and air (*i.e.*, void of favour before men, gods and demigods).

759

Searching, searching and searching, fretting (or being fatigued) and fretting, wandering, wandering and wandering till your head turns giddy. I saw that it is like beholding a puppet show.

760

Those that bear (see) us and those we bear (or see),knowing their deaths are at hand, and knowing our own, delusion suffers us not to know this. But her house deserted!

761

Though he read all that can be read and attain ample discrimination but how shall the hypocrite (consider) attain beatitude--like as the wandering wishes of a dog though lying at ease on the hearth.

762

If you seat a dog in a royal sedan, it cannot remain fixed in one mind. Thus cannot the man of ignorant mind restrain his soul.

763

Born on the earth, growing up in earth how shall a man quit the earth and attain heaven. The bliss of heaven does not exist in this earth.

764

What has the sage to do with rites? The sage requires no concealment; if the excellent man possesses undefiled wisdom he shall in this earth attain deliverance from all earthly ties.

765

He who offering erroneous prayers for wealth attain good works, through that wealth shall not attain honour. By honouring a teacher, he shall comprehend the greatness of the divine glory, and shine for .ever. (a loose version) 766

To be subject to (joined with) desire and avarice is a great grief. He that quits desire is the perfect man. If avarice leave thee thou shalt know the bliss of the next world.

767

Like him who, knowing the suitability of stones uniteth stones into a binding; if like him, thou know the desirable arrangement of thy mind and thus order thy mind--hereby shalt thou know the divinity and thenceforth live in happiness.

768

Bearing a load of (a toom full of) *jonna* a stupid bullock still wears a bell proudly on its neck; while it wears a bell and serves, blows follow it.

769

The excellence of him that is united with the deity is known to himself alone. How can others comprehend it? If he be himself become the God why should he worship him?

770

In the worship of God, in the temples, he showed us a path saying. There is the God. If ye understood it, this entire world is that deity which is origin of all the Gods.

771

All virtue combined became man, and he was produced; all sin combined, and woman (fiend) was born. Knowing woman to be evil, yet when ye see her ye fear to abhor her.

772

If a whore, faithful, comes perpetually she is not faithful but death. If death enters your house, will she not devour you?

773

If you do not put a basketful of bran before it, the she buffalo you have bought will not let you milk. He can you vainly love a dancing girl?

774

What does the arrogant high way man know of (care for poverty? As you call out for mercy he merely breaks your head) What does the young prostitute care about considering virtues of the faithful wife?

775

A house without a liberal man is a great demon street; a word void of wisdom is a blow with a stone; a loveless whore is a murderess.

776

He that says not thus large are her eyes, thus large her breasts, and who shines not thus entangled doth not desert devotion--this is the permanent sage.

777

This body is a leathern puppet with joints--a vessel full of lies. A shiftless whore, an entangled car--who can describe its abominations.

778

We must of necessity ramble as far as the mind rambles and must turn when the mind turns. He that roams and rambles--he seems as a God.

779

This is not a tattered cloth, says the recluse, but a fair vest; this is not a foul body but beatitude. Behold and wander at the greatness of him who is devoted to the Supreme.

780

Happy is he who without considering this or that place, everywhere dwells as Siva. To them of understanding he appears as a God.

781

Taking the flesh as a covering does the deceived creature devour flesh, If he were released from the flesh could he speak?

782

The talker shall in one way or another perish surely, the wise shall alone be happy and glorious in the earth; let disputes be ceased from and thus shall the yogee attain overwhelming ecstasy and thus gain perfection. (very hard) 783

Who are those that hear of or have seen the deity. Those who have heard of him alone see him. Gaze steadily on him whether in the form of ocean or any other.

784

Ignorant that the deity shines abroad in the earth, why should ye search imagining him elsewhere? That the deity exists within thee is truth.

785

Surely void of the creator exists not the creation The creator formed it diversely. Look to that external world. Look to that eternal world that is without creator.

786

He that perceiveth not him shall never become him. He who is in them is His. He that hath seen Him is himself the *yogee.*

787

Seeing the love of women sages (sanyasees) will love them, being immersed in the infamy of the world; when it has caught a bird, the cat is happy.

788

What does the dog know of the linga priests, God? What does the fox know of one meal a day and fasting? What does the obstinate fool know of the path of beatitude.

789

A pot without a bottom is unprofitable, a devotee without strength of body is useless. He has become like a shaven widow woman alas, alas.

790

It would be amazing if the ocean of six thousand paths should ever be so stirred up as to turn sweet. Though you should teach the knowledge of God in a thousand ways to a piece of wood, it would be vain, O Vema.

791

Though they search, they cannot discover that one God who alone is skilled in the scriptures; but the excellent man perceives Him in the earth. Him who is and is not, they cannot behold.

792

Ignorant of the true nature of inferiority and superiority, through desire ye perform salutations. Who is the honoured, which is the worshipper? What intrinsic difference exists?

793

If they see a sage, they who are bound in the ties of this world simply call him mad. They cannot quit their nature. If a fool should in this earth seek nature, shall he find it?

794

Men devoid of wisdom are indeed multitudinous, but though thou examine no man of wisdom is to be perceived. Through the deceptions of nature we cannot perceive the divinity.

795

When a plan is devised, unless it be performed, the hire is not given. Unless she satisfy your desire you would not give her a shilling. Thus is the teacher that bestows no beatitude is a son of apes!

796

When a pararamour takes one, is disgusted and leaves her; then (or afterwards), another takes and loves her. Will not dogs lick the leaf-plate that is tossed away after eating.

797

When we see a girl and exclaim how large are her eyes and how fair her breasts, the mind is deluded and falls in love, unable to perceive Him who dwells within our mortal frame.

798

He who through an airy nature falls in love is even ensnared by a girl with sunken eyes. He is born, lives, and again is born ceaselessly.

799

Growing by sucking the breast, he falls in love with the breast. By her breast, beatitude becomes insipid. He who will lave the breast is a saint forever.

* * *

800-899

800

Whatever creed we examine all are the creed of woman; besides, assuredly my creed is the creed of woman! For love is the aim of every enquiry. He who comprehendeth my creed he is the excellent.

801

When the husband; son--both (join) at once look at the wife's breasts with constant gaze; the husband looks with desire for the flesh upon it, the son for milk within it.

802

Being himself the son of another daughter the base wretch drives away his mother. Such blackguards are not produced even by boars.

803

By building chatrams (inns) at every step and by possession and wealth they increase their splendour; where ever they wander their shadow follows them; i.e., God will reward them.

804

You take a binding rope, bind and secure it. What theft has Lingadu stolen that he should be thus treated? Why is it that ye cannot be thus treated? Why is it that ye cannot see and worship the invisible atma linga?

805

To eat the *caraca* fruit (autaphrodisiac) and to bind his langoti tight, and to desert all women shew a vile nature. If thou bind it firmly (lit. pleasurably) to a twig, will an elephant remain fixed.

806

Musing on a sweet lip, we forget all wisdom; how shall the man of devotion know Thee. O God! Through a sight of the yoni shall we forget (Parama yogam) meditation on the supreme.

807

They cannot understand that there is but one God in the Siva, the Vishnu and all other creeds! Though these differ, can any diversity exist in truth (tatwa)?

808

Illusion (or death) is not an inconstant woman with glancing eyes, wearing beads and earrings and mounting on her husband's shoulder, she delays not to slay those who yield to her.

809

Nourishing matted locks, to cry shame on the world, to distort all the limbs and all yogeeism (devoteeism)--This is to seize the woman of beatitude and kiss her.

810

Who is unable to instruct the minds of those brutes clothed in human bodies who, while the mighty all exists within themselves seek him not within themselves but roam the earth to find him.

811

All those who pride on themselves on having bathed in the Ganges are defeated and consider their acts as mere vexation; surely the holy water of Vema's wisdom is nobler than the stream of Ganges and Gaya.

812

Mounting the steed of thy mind not knowing how to govern it perplexing it, why should the rider set out? Is Banares a dear friend of thine? Govern thy mind and thou shalt be independent of pilgrimage.

813

You put Siva, source of the Ganges, in the palm of your hand; and yet roam to the holy streams. This is like possessing butter and yet searching for melted butter.

814

Why go to Mecca? Why return thence? Is not the only lord here with us? Allah Mohammad universally exists in his fullness. (spreads undivided, animates unspurt)

815

The fool binds a linga to his throat, and this also being insufficient he climbs the mountain to visit the linga shine there at. Such a one can see beatitude?

816

They who knowing not the God who dwelleth in their body, wander and become tenants of the holy springs. These are like the ass that beareth about the sandal tree.

817

If thou perform bathing but give no charity thou gainest but the advantage of the plunge, void of instruction. Is not a fowl well versed in plunging in water?

818

O! ye! hypocrites, who ignorant of the revolution of time, continually perform the daily rites and (meditation) *japa*, what may be the path by which perfection is attainable through these rites and postures.

819

Some of these fools wander this starry land to worship. They go to Ramanatha (Rameswaram) and then suffer scorn. They go to Concan on pilgrimage but in truth merely to hear news that they had never heard.

820

By going a pilgrimage to Banares, and bathing on the Ganges ye indeed suffer hardship but shall never attain heaven. No more than a buffalo calf can resemble a cow by merely following about it.

821

If a fellow has gone to Banares what shall we say he has done? What if there had been something to cause his death and he had died on the road, his mind truly might still go to Kasi, but never can attain the better world.

822

If he who go to Kasi with great enthusiasm when by the wisdom of God they change their bodies, in transmigration he gives half his merits to his wife, and has only half to himself.

823

They who go to Kasi, get trouble and nothing else; why should ye roam merely to get an itching in your feet. Will not women also for hire get water and bear it about for hire?

824

A dog that has gone to Tirupati does not become a lion. A pig that goes to Kasi is no elephant. A whore that goes to the Sri Shylam is no modest woman.

825

Ceasing from food and sleep, a fool utterly void of understanding, for the sake of beatitude, roams the earth; he rambles like a mad dog.

826

He who calls himself a yogee, and gets together some of the components of yogeeism, and kills those who are in the world--that yogi who roams and robs men is no yogi but a (Ogu) vile wretch.

827

He who holds himself (a Paramahamsa) a perfect ascetic, by rarely wearing a dress and longs for the wealth of others 's no ascetic but (Parahimsa) death itself.

828

Postures and the like, bathings in the worship, pilgrimage to Kasi or a system of good works unless thou stay thy mind however many such paths thou walk, know that they shall avail you nothing.

829

They will journey on pilgrimages to Kasi and the bridge of Rameswaram. They can hereby behold piles of stones but not heaven, not even one of them.

830

If thou give food to Bramins, they say it will be profitable to thee; if you were to give it to dogs where would be the harm (inferiority)? They say that one soul resides (both here and there) in each.

831

The fool left his relations, bound himself with an iron langoti and quitting food and drink, and exceeded. If we give up the fluids of the body, can we attain perfection. How shall we have strength to worship?

832

Plunging, plunging and plunging in holy streams, squatting and squatting in meditation, talking and talking, charms becoming leaner and leaner, roaming, roaming, roaming and roaming from sanctuary to sanctuary--ye turn giddy and are ruined.

832

The impurities in the belly being the vilest of all, is the juice of food worse than that? Those therefore who fast, are fools unable to form comparisons.

834

He ignorant of the being that dwelleth in the body, wanders in other pilgrimages is a fool. Does not a jackass thus roam bearing a pack saddle.

835

That world hater (or recluse) who is attached only to using the words of stubbornness, no-where shall he attain the power of quelling death (yama). The recluse of the iron age is vile as the drinker of palm wine.

836

With their matted locks a fathom long, and their smearings of ashes, they forsooth are able to dispute the day with cupid himself and after all their very garments become the property (petticoats) of whores.

837

By a bald, head, and white streaks of ashes and postures, and airy diet, by all this a man is not a yogi unless his inner man be right.

838

If we look at the fine dresses (sects) they are marvellously foolish. Devotion does not hereby dwell in the soul. They merely form la startling appearance. They have neither the title nor the nature (viracti) of saints.

839

If you see among harmless cattle, one handsome ox with horns, it is indeed superior. But is wisdom attained by the mere shaven baldness of the sanyasi? (who only resemble helpless widows in this fancy) 840

The long windedness (lit. breath) of a fowl, the steadfast gaze of a frog--such follies are written by fate in the forehead of the devotee. This must surely befall him through his sins in a former birth.

841

If he rub ashes to his body and wear long locks, though he be a king he shall fail of heaven; however stiff a screen be, is it yet a door?

842

While all the precepts declare Siva to be the divinity, they seek and worship other deities; surely Bramins are in the path of destruction.

843

Hanging down their heads, void of the least patience opening and shutting his eyes and dumb--this is no wisdom but merely the residue of thy sins.

844

Woe to the world that is full of the destruction of souls. But first the woe to the Brahma! View all the Gods! Woe to them all.

845

They call Brahma the author of the writing of fate in our foreheads. Perhaps Brahma, who dwelleth in the lotus (wrote) destined that his own head should cleave to the hand of (Bhava) Siva! (Siva smote Brahma on one head which was separated and cleave to his hand.) 846

Those who believed in Siva have all become the share of the earth. Why then these disputes and discrimination of Gods. All the faithful to Vishnu have fallen to the shares of white ashes.

847

It is impracticable to dress oblations for however great a God, without imbibing the favour (or scent). Thus he has your leavings while ye talk of "devoting and setting aside as holy". Ye are still biting your lips at it.

848

The fool deceived becomes a devotee to Siva and submitted to slavish tasks. But the wise, an honoured, (badged) soldier is ever void of fear.

849

The skill of the laundress (who recognised the owner of each vest) is more than that of the bookworm. Better is a dog than Ganesha the dumpy king; noble is truth than all the Gods in the world.

850

If we know ourselves, the Veda would be all fooling to us; a mizzling rain is all folly to the store of grain; publish thou in the world O Vema that the six *sastras*, and the Puranas are mere infelicity.

851

All those of the race of Brahma are fallen creatures. Those of the race of Rishies are ruined. Will they call near them these hateful wretches nor detest them.

852

Consider the words of Vemana as those of a mad man. Some fall into channels and some into streams (proverb); but a small proportion of them are removed out of the (Veda Sastra) scriptural level.

853

In the thousand verses thus composed by Vemadu, many as are the bad, equally numerous are the good. Secrecy gives a charm to beauty and obscurity to wisdom; should not a lovely girl lie exposed naked on the couch.

854

Like mad foxes do the Bramins read the Veda perpetually howling it out. They know not its meanings. But Vemana knows the entire essence of the Vedas.

855

All *yagnas* were invented for the sake of discovering the fornications of a wife and the periodical ceremonies to the end of knowing a mother's adulteries In so vile a way was the chapter of ceremonies invented.

Note: At commencing the sacrifice called *yagna* the performer must require his wife to confess whether she has been untrue to him. The periodical ceremonies being performed to the late husband of a widow lead to the conviction, at least in her own mind, of her having been true or adulterous.

856

The height of excellence is to abstain from slaying. Thus say the Bramins, lords of earth and still commit slaughter of animals in sacrifice. Better is the *chandala* who devours dead cattle.

857

They pinch and scrub their halters (nose ropes) and rub themselves to remove all dirt, and pour water into their privities. By thus cleansing the whole body do they attain felicity.

858

Pauper Bramins meet together and recite babbling charms and talk saying they will perform the initiation of a boy into their caste. Like the crow that has drunk the washing of rice and goes on crowing.

859

Why take thy caste and pride thyself on it? Yea and what is the (twice born) Brahmin?

860

If ignorant of service how can they become slaves? Ignorant of the Vaishnava belief how can ye be Vaishnavite? While living, why do ye suffer burning like corpses? (i.e., smear yourselves with ashes) 861

If the pollutions caused by a birth or a death be real, and if the qualities communicated by that touch be destroyed to what end is it for a soul to become a hermit.

862

Shall the wicked, being produced through carnal desire, talking vainly, with false words and deceiving men and twisting about to get money, shall such a one become a teacher?

863

Unable to discern that this world is a delusion, some talk of the smock and some of the langoti. These are mere tricks of the privities.

864

The noble Brahmin goes to eat the vile funeral cakes of the ruined wretch. The Brahmin's wife haunts the marriage house; first they lose caste and then character.

865

In the night of ignorance doth the goddess of delusion wear her petticoat and conceal herself; in the daytime of wisdom, when about her work she looses her petticoat; this is no prostitute but an edged sword in the hand.

866

They are puffed up and cry I will perform a sacrifice, these who fill their bellies with the liquor vulva, these sons of whore brag nobly in their assemblies.

867

He calls men sudras and says begone thou sudra; this is a pariar worse than a pariar. If he says I am a twice born does he thereby become one?

868

Born and dying in ignorance of his prior state before all men, are they ensnared by their lusts? To what end do they leave wisdom and roam the earth.

869

These heroes--the Brahmins, Kshatrias and Vaisyas and Brahma, Vishnu and Siva all these are beasts. Ignorant of the divinity have they adopted forms thus diversified, 870

Defilement appears no where in the least but exists in our ideas; whoever considers it will see that the beauty of the world is in truth extreme. If thy ignorance depart, wisdom shall shine with thee.

871

Those who abuse the practice of wearing ashes on the forehead, that is, the Vaishnavites yet perform their funerals with fire and thus become the portion of the fire. They the Saivites who equally abuse the wearing of earth, by burying their dead become earth.

Thus the advantage of all their mutual abuse discovers itself in their shame,

872

However great the spell be, not even Brahma can utter it undefiled with spittle. But with what mouth is it they talk of spittle and defilement thereby.

873

While the fire in our body is ignited and burns, to what end do (the Vaishnavites) burn their corpses. By merely burning does he become mighty?

874

To put cord over the neck as the Lingamites and then to suppose that their soodra-ism has departed, this is mere (inferior sense) folly; if thy mind be not settled, will a cord give thee caste?

875

Wearing a silk vest and putting the Vaishnavite streak on their forehead, the Vaishnava sect has exalted its head in the earth. By the contrivance of numberless fopperies has the Vishnava sect been ruined.

876

If thou eat the body of a beast that eats pure grass they call you a pariar. Yet if he eat fowls and pigs (which are the foulest of feeders) a man is called wise.

877

If you go seasonably to the abode of Ranga (in the Cauveri) you will find the charming smell of toddy. Truly this is scorn of the lord of the world. (The Vaishnavites drink toddy while worshipping.) 878

In the house of the body a wild fire blazes with hunger; why should you burn your bodies? This is mere deception or perhaps this is punishment inflicted on the Dasoos. (This is a sneer at Vaishnavites.) 879

They find fault with the well used by the village and are delighted with the water in which a holy man's feet have been washed. What profit is there in foot washings?

880

Those who understand omens and the interpretation of moles, are not to be met with in the Iron age. For their own profit men will explain the virtue of these. In cases where fortune meets us, these are accepted as its tokens.

881

A parcel of old whores (windows) join together in this age and through devotion to Siva forsooth go on dancing. Shall such hypocrisy obtain them felicity.

882

He who cannot at first apply himself to restrain his passions, when he dies, seeks to become a devotee; void of purity of heart, how should beatitude appertain to him.

883

He who has learnt to die, all his turning sanyasi is merely as though he at last lost his caste; the sin of doing this alone is certain. There is no ulterior profit in it.

884

The leaving (spittle) of a pretty white dog are pure in our eyes. The spittle of a young dancing girl is acceptable to us. These vile leavings are precious everywhere. Then why are the leavings of those we love evil in our sight.

885

However much you wash it well, (does) the defilement of the mouth depart? That alone is a mouth (which does not speak falsehood); that daily speak falsehood is not a mouth but a mouth below.

886

Binding the linga fairly on their body, but unable to fix his faith on that lingam, failing of beatitude, they perish in their folly.

887

All those who trust in Vishnu fall to the share of white earth; to what end are these disputes and sects (dissensions) in religion. The Lingadharies become the portion of earth, 888

When he proceeds from his mother's womb, had he a lingam along with him? Then what a joke it is for him to wear one afterwards.

889

The Vaishnava sect puts on a silk turban and silk vest, and is puffed up in the earth. These are mere semblances and the emptiness of the Vaishnava creed,

890

Unable to know the great secret, they continue and frame religions, and merely give sorrow to each other, like as a dog that is agitated at the sight of a mirror,

891

You see that those endowed with form all possess the first image. Why should ye value this man or that as a superior. If ignorant of this principle, how shall he attain happiness?

892

A pariar eats flesh, all other people eat fat--are not they one caste? They do not see that all castes are in fact one.

893

Why dost again and again abuse a pariar? Are not his blood and flesh and thine one? Of what caste is he who is immingled with him? The deity animates his entire works.

894

When people see those who wear ashes they imagine that they contract inequity from them. When they see the Namadharies (Vaishnavities) they consider it healing. What are the ashes, and what the white clay (of the Vaishnavites) in the eyes of the supreme.

895

Those who are divided into sects are ten thousands. This is merely for filling their bellies--they cannot see the divine spirit. Can cranes however many they assemble, devour ships?

896

By slaughtering the animals that eat grass men become pariars in the earth. But what sort of caste is that, that eats pigs and fowls (as the respectable classes do) that devour the dung of all?

897

If men in the earth choose to take pipe clay and soften it well, then put it smoothly on their foreheads it is merely a mark, and thereby men cannot become Vaishnavites.

898

Though thou put on the mark and call thyself a (servant) *adiya* as the Vaishnavites do and eat chewed pawn, bow down and call thyself a *Dasee*-- This is all merely a means of subsistence but no ground for happiness.

899

We see that men are like barber's basin, common to all; then, while they thus are mingled, why babble about their castes. Put thy right hand on their heads and expose this to their ridicule,

900-999

900

See how the Locomotives (jangams) eat immovable creatures. How animals eat vegetables of many different tastes. Then all animals soon eat themselves, O Vema! (Note the verbs are masculine), 901

If we go on worshipping (shactis)the demigods, what is the use of men any more in the earth. Think not it is a sin but seize and punish them all who in the world are men of virtue.

902

Why should they who worship the (jeeva linga) living principle still think of stone figures? When ye have tasted delicious sugar will ye again taste what is bitter?

903

What is the use of wearing an empty lingam and painting your body with ashes; If you consider it closely--if you wash yourself and wear a lingam, will it fill your belly in any way?

904

After bathing, fasting, preparing food and desiring the god to eat it, they smite him on the face and devour it themselves. (satire)

905

Men imagine stones to be Siva, and magnify them. Stones are stones and not Siva. Why is it that we cannot discern Siva who dwells within us?

906

When a man comes up as evidence the court will be displeased with him, so if thou avoid all inconsistency, if thou neither diminish nor add to it. All other evidence is no evidence.

907

Like as a pearl is produced united with *tunga* grass, like to a wishing tree growing before thy house, like as though the cow (camadhenu--the celestial cow) were born in thy presence, thus fortunate was the birth of Vemana in the world!

908

He who knowing the Everlasting considers Vemadu as Siva in his mind and cautiously guardeth his heart; this is the man of unfluctuating mind.

909

Are not all they who read the whole *shastras* on a level with those who do not read them, if from the mouth of the teacher they learn not true application (enjoyment)? Hear this word openly declared to the world!

910

He who can gainsay the writing of Brahma, he who can destroy the institutes of the Prime Vishnu, he who can stand in opposition to Him who has three eyes such shall never appear among men, save (excepting) thyself O! Vema!

911

Fate continually awaiteth all men however great; is it a marvel when debasement comes? Did not Vishnu who bore the mountain Govardhan on his finger, afterwards float in peril on a banyan leaf?

912

Siva, the chief of Gods, though he burnt up cupid with the flame of his forehead eye cannot leave his wife; who then are the chiefs of sages who can desert woman?

913

Ah! did you never hear that golden animals (deer) are produced in the world? Is king Rama devoid of sense? Your schemes avail nothing for fate rules all.

914

When Dasaratha thought to crown his son Rama king of earth being deluded he bound his head with merely matted hair. Thus intentions avail nothing, For fate rules all.

915

Did the amorous Hara (Siva) fail of becoming mighty? Did not the amorous Vishnu become mighty? If Ganesa who hated love become great?

916

With the army of monkeys that wandered the hills without food, Rama king of earth formed an army and conquered. But one Vibhishana ruled Lanka by the favour of Lakshmi.

917

When Siva struck off and threw away Brahma's head, did any of the other deities oppose him? Who can perfect the sinner who hath not the favour of Siva?

918

Though his dwelling be on Meru, the golden hill cupidity will not leave the God Indra himself. Did not he ask Karna for his armour and large earrings?

919

He, Vishnu, that lay down in the sea of milk, why should he have wished for the milk of the shepherd's village? How sweet is the property of our neighbour?

920

Did not Indra, through cupidity become degraded? Was not cupid, through desire, turned into earth? When Brahma contracted desire did not he lose his principal head.

921

Cubera (Dhanapathi *i.e.* Plutus) being his friend, and united to him (the points of heaven they rule, touch and they are friends) how did Siva become a mendicant? However numerous your rich friends be, no wealth but your own can aid you.

922

In dress you may become a *Dasari*, when the due season is lost, you may become a *Jangam*, ascetic. But though then thousand things happen to you, you cannot become a Brahmin.

923

By the various names of generative eggs, having grown like hills, recklessly (dancingly, lit) they insult God When their turn arrives they fall in the hands of Yama's messenger.

924

Rama did not consider whether there were golden deers in the world or not? What is Rama so insance a prine? *(sic.)* If you leave your town and roam in the forests your senses will not remain.

925

One Siva carried a woman Parvathi on his side; one Brahma held a woman, Saraswathi in his mouth. One Vishnu bore a woman, Lakshmi, on his breast; for woman they thus suffer great trouble.

926

Though he hath the hills of silver and gold, Kailasa and Meru, why doth the god Siva wander and collect alms. His neighbour's property is sweet to every man however great.

927

King Sibi cut a piece out of his body to give for a dove to a hawk. He became the topic of report and attained fame. They will not esteem him who is wicked, but will praise him who is charitable.

928

Vishnu left the circle of skin, and would not come to the shore being entangled in the wiles of Lakshmi, daughter of the sea. Vishnu (Shargnee the Bowyer) being so mighty, what can men do?

929

He that is as great as Sukrachari, knowing all things with his sharp sight if instead of restraining his mind let it roam, is like the blind crow. (The crow and Sukrachari each have but one eye) 930

What king is mightier than (Duryodhana) Dhartarashtra? He and all the rest are dead, All the wicked shall surely suffer a violent death.

931

King Dasaratha when on earth, thinking it was an elephant (this is a story in Raghuvamsa) slew the son of the guru in the earth (or cast him down to the ground); through grief for his son was not his life also ended? (lit. his going was extinguished.) 932

Pandu, king of earth, slew the couple of animals (deer) through ignorance. Thereby how long did he live in the world, and what did he (eat) enjoy?

933

No man's acts can be transferred to another. God took the just king to an unsuitable place and changed, him into Kanku Bhatlu, alas, alas!

934

Kaika (Kaikeyi) one wife of Dasaratha and mother of Bharata was born to cause the ruin of Rama's City. Seeta was born to destroy the state of Lanka and they say Chitrangi was born to destroy the king.

935

Surely the evil of poverty is an interminable degradation. Thereby king Nala left his palace. For a mere joy will they suffer such distress.

936

When we are born, before they seize and cut the navel; when we were born, god, the teacher was born in this world. Examine well and know this.

937

Though you be a hero, or have learned wisdom, or learnt reading, or be at court, beatitude will not reach you. It is the fruit of birth and you cannot attain it even by austerities.

938

In the belly of Vishnu the world shineth (see Bhagavat-geeta). In it existeth all the universe. All the millions of animated are hence evidently Vaishnavites.

939

Still do they speak calling the world, illusion. It is no illusion. It is formed of the divinity. If this be delusion, tell me where the actual divinity is to be found.

940

Behold! Brahmins, Kshatrias, Vysyas, Soodras, even Brahma, Vishnu and Siva--these are beasts. In ignorance of the divinity have all these forms originated.

941

Produced before the water and germinating in water, that germ fills the world. Learn that this water is the world (mystic).

942

Hast thou not heard that Vishnu and the other god (Brahma) are dead? Hast not thou heard that Siva sports alone in varying forms through all religions. Hast thou not heard of those studies that have an aim. Reflect and know the season when thy day shall come, select the noblest and most stable pursuit.

943

Ye who will not consent to give your women in marriage to all the (total) men of all castes, ye yet agree to take their daughters in marriage. O ye vile Brahmins!

944

His mother is Gowri (Parvati). His father is Shambhu (Siva). The troops of lower deities are all his relations. The house of his birth is the glorious Cailasa.

945

Using the terms mother and father they know not the truth being produced from the Yoni and Lingam. But know thou that the mother is Vishnu and the glorious Siva thy father.

946

Those men of wisdom, who begin by subduing their mind and thus live shall at last see the abode of bliss. If thou plant a tree shall not thou surely obtain its fruit.

947

If thou know the real nature of noble Shaiva calling (profession), walk in the knowledge of God. Though shall be as though born as of a tiger and lion.

948

They who revile Siva all wear the attire of Vyasa and Dakhsa Prajapati and the rest are shameless like a man who knowing the evils of fornication and yet committing it.

949

The Shaiva creed is the most acceptable speaker of all the six creeds. Men cannot comprehend that God is one. The discrimination of persons exists in our fancies not in the deity.

950

Unless our desires be quenched, our body being set on fire will be vexed. Let us not be tossed about in this house of the body, but know that Siva exists in the body.

951

Siva is the radical root in the world. (if thou consider it) What they call Vishnu shines as being Siva. Siva is Vishnu. O ye who wear the semblance of Siva and Vishnu.

952

In this vile (Kaliyuga) Iron age while all petty rogues (thieving plow boys) make a sport of all faith in Siva, shall this hypocritical profession attain salvation?

953

Those scholars in the Veda who are versed in the *Veda-shastra*, and the sciences, search and seek for thee, but cannot perceive thee in the earth. Finally they fall dead, O Vema!

954

When Brahma with all his reading was destroyed and when the original Vishnu was (ended) slain, then Vemana exposed their emptiness. (let sought their disgrace.)

955

Vemana has surpassed the Vedas. Vema is the Vedanta. The Vedas are all different. Meddle not with the contentions about such matters.

956

Have ye not heard of that men of trifling minds (entangled) confused by the intricate Five letters (Namassivaya) and five Vedas (4 Vedas and fifthly the puranas). In the five sects, if thou consider it, Siva dwells.

957

If poor in wealth a man retains not resolution. By poverty king Nala lost his home, gave his garment to a bird and was ruined.

958

The God-like force (or the force of the Veda) that Dasasyu (Ravanasura) being mighty gained, being mightier than any whom even the Gods had beheld, perished by the means of mere monkeys and all his tribe sunk with him.

959

Through the words of his wife Kaika the king (Dasaradha) perished. For the sake of a woman (Seeta) the name of *Dasasya* (Ravanasura) was humbled. Surely every mean act, who ever he be, shall follow him.

960

That one like Brahma should have been destroyed. That one like cupid should have turned into flame. Then shall ye who are with a sure life live as though eternity were yours?

961

The original Purana is such as slays the Rakshrsas. The Bharata and others are of kin (i.e. benevolent as relations.) The Gurupurana is the destroyer of imposture.

962

Among the Gods Brahma, Siva, Vishnu and the rest and among the demiGods that roam the three worlds and among the excellent men and with in thyself O Vema he who acts up rightly is the eternal.

963

The Lingam is the highest Siva. The (Zangam) worshipper, is the animated beast. If that animated being be pure, he shall attain Siva, Unless thou know the unknown, how shalt thou attain the divinity.

964

Then thou hast with (sport) joy perceived the lingam in thy body, thy mind shall be enamoured of that lingam. If thou fix (or restrain) thy mind, in it. shall the lingam dwell.

965

Through ignorance of the secret of our patron (or loved) Linga, the eager fool wanders to the Hill of Shrishylam. At last he fails of bliss and becometh a fool.

966

Born in a human race, and growing up there from the day he was born in it the man devoted to Siva becometh noble. (lit. rich)

967

He that is born in a human race and who grows up there in becometh a man; hear this--who is the noblest in the race of men? He who walks in the sect of Siva, this is the chief of the noble.

968

The Smrities all declare Siva to be the chief Brahma. How is it then that Brahmana pays adoration to any other. Should not we call those who believe in Siva, Bramins?

969

Were fire a deity, by worshipping it should not we attain the dwelling of salvation? Did not the fire turn pale before Veerabhadra.

970

Were not the men destroyed (turned into water) who held fire in their hands and reviled Siva, Do not ye know the troubles that happened at the sacrifice made by Dakshudu?

971

He wears the lingam merely to attain money, thereby, vile and worthless son of a brute. Being for the sake of money they fall into the doctrine of works.

972

The firmament is in our eight sides. The heaven is widely extended in every part on our eight quarters. In the midst of that ineffable firmament the divinity is mightily infused.

973

Vishnu and Siva dwelling perpetually in the soul of a foolish mind is he who seeks for a distinct deity. Like a shepherd who seeks the sheep that is under his armpit.

974

What is the use of a linga that is tied and dangles at your neck and is not let go. Heaven is the witness to the entire world.

975

What is called Veda is in fact mere dispute. Vishnu and Siva are both combined in the Veda. That existeth every where. There is neither difference nor distinction; praise him.

976

False is their creed who declare (in the world) that it is greatly profitable to give up the enjoyment of this life. Can ye not see that the next world shines forth in the present life.

977

That saint who hath learnt to know the difference between sunshine and shade cannot live in this world which he despises from knowing a better, but the glutton saint who worships the belly ever roameth the earth.

978

Truly they call a goldsmith a thief. He is thief who calls him thief. Did not *Vishvakarma* convert earth into gold and share it out?

979

The Linga creed is the noblest of the six creeds. There is none superior in the world and there is no thief greater than the linga worshipper. (weaver)

980

Sandhya performed out of season is mere idling. What is time? What is the preceding time? If thou rule not time, and past time how is this Sandhya?

981

If thou see him (the supreme being) who slew Brahma the lotus born who plunged Vishnu into the (ambudhi) sea, who sent Siva to remain fixed on the hill of Cailasa, if thou see him being thyself transformed into Siva, thou shalt attain the highest of joy.

982

Whether you name it Siva, Indivisible the chief spirit, the Lingam or living lingam, the terms indeed vary, but the divinity is all one.

983

The curse of Goutama is terrible as the wrath of Siva, the poison throated. It made Indra king of Gods, as a debased. The reproach of Goutama the *muni*, was an infallible magic arrow. (Sanscrit) 984

If a misfortune befalls Siva the forehead eyed, let even the wisest condole with him and remove it (teercu). If, knowing it to be a scorpion you seize it will it own your kindness and not sting you? (That is, meddle not to comfort a passionate violent person.) 985

There is one creation possessing redness, whiteness and blackness; great in might unknown to anyone possessing power. He that has acquired power to view this divinity is himself a part of it.

986

Brahma is merciless. Mighty as they were, Parashara (father of Vyasa) and the rest were burnt up. What then are the senseless wretches void of wisdom (*Vivara*).

987

There was once a merchant who for a wonder in this earth knowing the deity performed every virtue, and became celebrated. But failing of reverencing Yama he drew near to Siva.

988

Both the evil and the good done by us in a former birth regularly become our portion in this life. How should either good or evil that we have not done in the first birth betide us?

989

Why did Sesha, king of serpents gnash his teeth with rage. Why did Surya through anger become cruel? By anger Vulkan became diminished in day light. Anger is unprofitable to any man.

990

Him that we call the Teacher is unknown to these men; in a thousand ways is Brahma the ruler. He is Lord of Earth and Teacher of all. Thus esteemed, who is his equal, where shall we see him?

991

If thou view and look close thou shalt know that after thou hast put on a mortal body and provided the seven sons (i.e., the seven chief good deeds) and afforded protections to thy kith and kin, thou shalt derive no advantage from them.

992

Is a man now able himself to alter that writing of fate that Brahma originally wrote on his forehead; who on earth is now able to know the cupidity of the avaricious soul?

993

Brahma is the writer of destiny, Vishnu is the Minister (counsellor). Siva is the original agent. View this distinctly. If thou understand the conduct of these three and likewise their original (i.e., the supreme spirit) then shalt thou become a worshipper of the chief of beings.

994

Among those three Hara, Hari and Aja (Brahma) which is scaler (lit., seat), That is creator which is the chief (Vishnu who as Krishna turned thief) which is the original? Who can name each of these appropriately and without confusion?

995

Behold there are three (Trimoorties) Images. There are also three fools (Ravanasura in the Ramayana, Duryodhana in the Bharata, Kansa in Bhagavata), Those who have excelled their equals are three (Rama over Ravanasura, Bheemudu over Duryodhana, Krishna over Kansa). Of these which is most glorious, which the inglorious, estimate their worth and explain it, O Vema!

996

Looking upon all creatures as equal knowing the course of that pair, birth and death; finally thus shall not. He punishes several. Then is there a more righteous judge than Yama?

997

All men consider Yama as a great sinner, and reproach him well and greatly, What does Yama commit even the smallest evil?

998

However often we talk of that day or once upon a time (i.e., a former birth) it is no nearer to the present. Talking of the present does not make it the past. Then know the difference of these, do not become a jest. But know that the three a. e one. This shall gain the heaven. (Possibly the three are the Trimoorties).

999

These aching (teasing) bones are the rafters. The entwined nerves are the laths. The strong skin may be considered the covering ail. The doors are the nine apertures. With pride the five (senses or pranas) if we go to look at them have exceeded through cause of hungers and thirst. In the body, like to a vest, the strong family of consanguinity dwells. His acts are the covering cast over all. In this house imbued with the nature of dung and urine and in such a dwelling how shall we dwell? The firm sage alone knows that which is fixed and permanent.

* * *

1000-1099

1000

If you one day put your anus in your hand and wash it, what have you gained? How much so ever you wash the scales off your teeth, will its stink ever depart?

1001

Of gifts, the gift of food is the noblest. In music, the melody of the *Sama Veda* is the sweetest, In meditation that of Siva is the noblest.

1002

Burn him, Burn him, cries Pluto. This is more talking like a magpie. He cannot see what the truth is (that he is himself but a component part of creation). They who participate in the deity cannot themselves see god.

1003

Let us adore and glorify the (Pranalinga) prime spirit. But for what offence do ye bind it about your neck. Joy (i.e., the deity) is a witness to us of this folly.

1004

Wearing ashes of things that are bhavi (i.e., not lingamite) he calls this a form of Siva devoid of shame. But surely all animals are gifted with the linga. (Ye are as proud as a dog with two).

1005

Stupid fools are they who hide their wealth in the earth, and again dress their food in the earthen vessel of the body. Why should ye be so foolish for this muddy life?

1006

To the whole of the Siva sect, Hari is Teacher (by a refined explanation) and Hara (Siva) is Teacher, to the Hari creed. What sort of teacher is the wretch void of qualities of excellence.

1007

He that is unborn (Aja, Brahma) shines betwixt Vishnu and Siva, and in the midst of these does the *yoni* shine; It possesses a peculiar *kala* which however is unperceptible.

1008

When one life is past the fool shall again be born; again shall he love and again feel affection; again shall he roam the countries and villages like to a homeless monkey.

1009

How long does the soul, unprotected continue to die and be born again naturally (sahaja is born with us). To live without forgetting him is perfection,

1010

When all those who talk of the high deity as in unity, are freed from the body, then shall they be secure from sorrow and sin and enjoy happiness.

1011

To know the nature of the fluctuating and that of the changeless, is in the power of astrologers; who can inspect the body? Like as the swan is said to discriminate between water and milk.

1012

In the five faces of Siva the five letters (na-ma-si-va-ya) produced; by them is the world supported. Then how is it that they fail to praise the Five Faced.

1013

The Goddess of Earth as they call her is clay, seeing that all men know how that Goddess was produced, she became very weighty, They even call that Goddess equal to Siva as sustaining all.

1014

Lime is the best of all matters. Lime displays the present world in the earth, and it also shows us heaven.

1015

If thy good acts be great they shall not pass away; alas surely fate in a fitting place changed Dharmaraj into Kanku Bhattu.

1016

He puts his gift into the hand and pours the water of donation; thus doth he make fitting benefactions; but knows not that he and that of his neighbours are one. (Each is a form of Eswara.)

1017

They muse on the mantras but know not their meaning; ignorant of that signification they become blind. To become reborn and great let him learn it from the Teacher.

1018

Maya, that is, Vishnu--is there any other to whom the name applies? 'Cupid' is the dear son (son of kisses) of Maya; in Maya do his powers originate.

1019

Vishnu, he who hath a burnt body, he, Siva with the burnt throat, Brahma who smeareth over his body--these are allies. When the three thus meet it is a joy to the world.

1020

Let us not trust him who walks in another path; consider even his vest as a species of evil. It is the form of Ravanasura well known.

1021

Gadheyudu (Viswamitra, son of Gadhi) formed a world in imitation of that formed by Brahma and unable to know the truth gained (he gained only his pain). Doth the angry man know himself?

1022

Do not Siva (Shambhudu) slay and restore his son Viswamitra to life. Did not Vishnu revive his son Manmatha? The Vedas give numberless meanings of these stories.

1023

A thousand and thousands of the leaders of fishes who caused the Vedas (nigama) to float on the sea, to churn nectar beneath that hill did he place three thousand firm tortoises, a thousand tens of Krishnas to see the shepherdesses in the shepherds' hamlet, four thousands of Narasimha incarnations to tear the breast of the Rakshasas, to slay Ravanasura, ten thousand Ramas, Parasuramas, ten thousand--if thou ask where is Siva, He who in the form of Vishnu underwent the incarnations. He dwelleth in Kasi.

1024

If the teachers be ruined is not the whole caste destroyed? If Brahmins be destroyed he shall turn to ashes. If thou destroy Hara and Hari far is beatitude from thee.

1025

Our limbs to the God of fire, the bones, when burnt to the Goddess of earth, the excess of wealth to the kings, the entire soul to lovers, stubbornness to fools--the Sankara Vismriti to pariars and to the great avenger (Pluto) wrath belong.

1026

In whatever direction each man's desire is, in proportion to his desire, shall Vema cause them to attain the blessings of this and the next world. By the favour of Siva shalt thou render them acceptable, O Vema.

1027

They think on the mantras, but know not their meaning. How are those twice born who are ignorant of the meaning. He who comprehends the signification this is the only Bramha Rishi.

1028

The wild melon leaf is still more poisonous than the margosa. The heretical prathama shakhi (sectory) is more venomous than a serpent and a black complexioned Brahmin is worse poison than musk.

1029

By not quitting the assertions (violence) of the eight creeds, the holy have all become ruined. If you hold dung in your hand why cleanse it externally.

1030

Soul and the divinity exist in full force in the (diverse) forms that are in this world. But the Jangams, ignorant of this, cannot find the path.

1031

What means "Bramin", what means "devotee", what means "enjoyer", what means donor--however diverse their names, Plato's realm is their portion.

1032

Those of the Bouddha sect consider the intellect to be the divinity. They reckon, with degraded minds which is highest and which lowest. They have left of discriminating both good and bad, the vile calves.

1033

The unholy wretch who joins the skull-sect is ignorant of the beginning and the end of life; and in folly reviles Siva, alas he is ruined, (This sect is atheistical and epicurean. They deny both creation and destruction.)

1034

Likewise, by the Shacta creed, men consider power to be the divinity and, void of all sense (fitness) they fully perform the rites of pariar generations.

1035

What sort of caste is that of Rishies? Enquire and know; they became lovers of God. They became the divinity. Finally however great they be they are devoured by the funeral flame.

1036

Born in the *rishi* tribe, thereafter they are exalted in the *gotra* (tribe). They are not descended from Brahma, how then should they be Brahmins?

1037

Those sinful ones who undertake to walk in luxury eating and resting, and hard conduct--these shall not escape being bound in hell and cast into the mills of Yama.

1038

The life we enjoy shall not pass in all one manner; wealth and poverty await us all in this iron age; even Hari, Hara and Aja look upon evil and good as one.

1039

Holding Siva the Lord, the body to be his temple, and attaining rest, he who uniteth his soul with Siva, this is the Siva-yogi.

1040

Brahma has given wealth to one man and a liberal disposition in the mind to another. May Brahma perish and his wife's marriage cord be broken at the wharf.

1041

On the day when the term expired, it is impossible even for the three (Gods) to continue without suffering death. Why do ye dread the limit? Is the life eternal? It is brief, O Vema!

1042

Why did Brahma bestow a delightful odour in a ball of ashes; what fault (falsehood) had gold committed before him? Let the widow of Brahma have her cord broken at the wharf.

1043

He made the waters of the sea salt. He made the man of wealth avaricious. The acts of Brahma are acts of ashes.

1044

Beholding the craft of women, Bhairu Siva (Dog headed) refrained from marriage. So did the Big-bellied. Anjaneya (Hanuman) from his birth bound his *langoti* tight.

1045

Time and fate are boundless. Let us not oppose them but conduct ourselves as they lead us here on earth. Leave Brahma (Vidhi) in his eternal sleep and dream. O! ye idiots all! walk; O! men in the ways of beatitude.

1046

While you perform the worship of the shakti (inferior Goddesses) how should the Savitri (holy verse, Gayatri) continue on the earth? Sin is produced. Do not seize and punish it.

1047

If a noble person comes and kills a cow, his crime-can by no means be evaded, and at last, he is surely to Yama as a goat bound for sacrifice.

1048

The sun and the moon are present. The wind, fire and peacock spangled. Divinities are before thee. The earth and air are present. So many divinities are before thee. If thou wilt require, O Vema!

1049

Why marry? Why beget children? Why suffer this sorrow? It is madness! Like as though a man lifted a rock upon his head.

1050

The Divinity Himself became the universe. and was born when he hungers he shall eat this universe with desire (lit, its noble juice), In contradiction to his former acts he shall devour and destroy it. Alas! what do they call this?

1051

The Deity became man, he became woman leaving sorrow and having those desires that never relinquish in each age he is born. O ye wise! behold this noble object of meditation.

1052

In the various tribes of animals the deity was repeatedly reborn; like as if confused he roamed and roved; were we to call this body eternal? Would not the deity laugh?

1053

Who is the living man? Who is he who bore him? Who is the dead? No one knows this course! He that is, who produceth, who dieth, is one divinity.

1054

United with every living creature, manifest is the deity within them. Consider this deity carefully, whether it is female or male?

1055

Born, he existeth, unborn he existeth not, awhile he dieth; awhile lives again, This is the mere diceplay of Brahma! Nothing is stable!

1056

Why first are we born? Why die at last? Why troubled by reason of the ruthless Yama? Restrain thy mind from longing for birth.

1057

However great he be, to let the great sinner duly attain salvation there is one expedient at the time of death; let him give up all his desires, and think on God. Thus shall he become beatified.

1058

Though you impress his image on thee or name thyself his son, or eat his betel spittle serving him abjectly, shall any thing be attained by thee beyond thy destiny?

1059

Entangled in vain desires, observing the lives of consanguinity, a man becomes mad and roams the world. Where are our fathers and mothers? What are they? and what do they for us? (lit. why they to us?)

1060

The hill monkey has (if you look) the monkey for a (pērantālu) wife; a banda (a poor king) for a minister; (Banda--a beggar who tortures himself to extort alms from fools). Look at the Banda; villainous slanderers are his kin.

1061

Ignorant of the term set to the expenditure of life, it is fit for no one to write or cause to write at any time or in any place never write.

(This folly signifies that what is rendered permanent by writing may become false.)

1062

He who duly reverences Bramins and the Gods, who justly governs the earth, and thus gains wealth, which he spends in liberality, he, thus looking to the path to the beatitude, and has love to God. This is a king!

1063

Consider the spittle (leavings) of flies, of courtesans--they are acceptable to men and gods. Then why is our own spittle unacceptable to us?

1064

All wealth that is buried falls to the share of the earth; all that is out falls into the hands of others; all that we eat is the gain merely of straining inner system; what is bestowed alone remains ours.

1065

Give or not give, hope will bestow; however unsuccessful we still hope. Give or not give, it gives the world. Examine and see this. In this there are no free agents.

1066

Becoming a foetus it will remain in the womb for a few days. Thereafter it will surely not remain. The foetus is born in the earth; the foetus is the protection of the spirit in the earth, O Vema!

1067

Foulness in the belly, masses of flesh, bones--if you view it there is but a filthy skin over it. What manner of dwelling is this? What manner of comfort is this?

1068

If we eat not food, the fire in the belly devours the impurities of the belly. Thus if he abstain from food, he who fasteth devoureth impurity.

1069

If the *Carnam* be a low fellow, the farmers will all join and tell him to bow down whenever they have a mind. But if the *Carnam* be firm, we are your children, say they.

1070

A cat that listens a squeak is annoyed, if while eating its food it sees one of its own species (caste). He that hath no caste is considered a god in the world (as impartial).

1071

A fellow on one leg is no saint. If one carries cow-dung she is no slut, if one sees either of these he is merely astonished (his eyes redden).

1072

In the Linga sect, a set of hypocrites has arisen and these having handsomely reviled one another are all turned to dust by the Turk tribe to whom their discussion render them easy converts.

1073

A man is distinguished in the world, and becoming himself a great *somayaji* is born, a brother to the village god Potarazu. But you may consider him as merely the vile goddess of death to the rams that are sacrificed.

1074

He who saith this (external) figure is thy form and beholdeth in his internal image, Him that is worthy to be wore slipped of all worlds. In that form in which he himself exists shall he behold the Lord.

1075

He that hath not subdued (slain) his mind as we still further consider, is lower than a pariar, O man! death (naraka) shall befall (lit. come to) him after death.

1076

The chariot has five linch-pins; when the charioteer propels, the car proceeds. The car of thy body has five linch pins the senses); seek him who evidently guides it.

1077

Those wretches (lives) that artfully destroy animals while either sleeping, drinking waters or standing still and singing shall at the end in the same manner perish.

1078

Becoming free thinkers and ruined just like crows roaming the land wandering without understanding in them, they devour dung and urine; they die and become a part of earth.

1079

That house that we call the body do we daily sweep, smear with cow-dung, plaster, and order; at last we quit it and depart, so deceitful (or fleeting) is the soul.

1080

To what end is all this reading, to what end are all these disputations? If thou wouldest remain of one mind, thou shouldest become an accomplished sage and attaining absorptions become thyself, the Universe.

1081

Surely these vile tenets (Veda) are mere contention. The words of Vemana are knowledge (Veda). Verify none can show you any good. Though good were taught, you would not do it. If a man did well this would be the perfect man.

(సుండీ is a vocative plural of which సుమీ is the singular.)

1082

Like as camphor, burnt in fire loses its fine smelt. Thus the fragrance of wisdom in the debased can attain no nobility.

1083

He who knows the truth knows the Divinity and this will enable him to slay all his lust (literally vigours). Will he who has swallowed a delicious plantain swallow venom?

1084

Wonderful is it that the millions of animated beings should behold the great spirit, if thou consider in thy heart.

1085

Sorrow originates in impurity of heart. Like as the sun shines on all nature, pure water is in the sanctified body.

1086

Ye who first drove away all your original Gods, ye who drove away the succeeding deities, smite with the slipper your present paltry divinities.

1087

He who has beheld all the glory that is concealed within the veil, and has also fixed his mind on the divinity, that mighty saint who existeth in exalted holiness, at where shall we seek him?

1088

To know myself is to know thee How should he who knoweth not himself know thee. Let us learn from Boya Caannappa the prayer that teaches a knowledge of ourselves and thee (easy and useful in grammatical construction).

1089

That deity that alone comprehendeth the scriptures is found by constant seeking The Lord seeketh the man that seeketh him. Are there any who are wise and have learnt to seek him?

1090

If we love him, he will love us. If we love not him he will not love us (in the world). All our gorgeous apparel any our devils are all of no avail in the world.

1091

Without self possession the mere favour of learning will never remove the doubts of the aspirant. No more than darkness will be dissipated by a painted flame.

1092

By gentleness every object is pleasantly attained. It is a true victory; by it our vows are performed, I will lay you any bet. How great were the difficulties that Dharmaraj conquered by means of gentleness? (admirable and easy),

1093

When the men of this world see the exalted saint they will censure him but cannot comprehend him. What difference can the hand perceive between nectar and any other taste.

1094

From his birth onwards how many diverse evil thoughts the sinner entertains. Like to a lame dog that is in imagination eating meat.

1095

If he have learnt to speak prudently (lit. knowing abstracts), why should we consider his youth or age? May not a letter written by a child be respectable?

1096

Continuing to live and see (as in houses), listening to modes contrary to sense, do men pass away like an old song, listening to this they go on and go on and become a tale.

1097

As they who have lost their eyes or legs seek each others aid, and as the beggar unites with beggar alone. Thus wealth and poverty associate together.

1098

Is not the dying of some of our kin before our eyes an evidence/to us? Can we look upon our frail lives as eternal?

1099

Like as the lamp of the sun enters into water, thus does the eye behold the deity. Like as the glistening of the soil of the desert in the mirage.

* * *

1100-1199

1100

If we kill, sin is contracted; by not slaying virtue attaches But to the omniscient, whether he slay or save, neither attaches. How can that death be slain that thus slay Siva? (a very difficult grammatical construction to translate).

1101

You may straighten a tree to prevent its being crooked. You may duly rectify stone but you cannot straighten the mind that it become not more crooked.

1102

Whatever any one at any time advises, a man should listen to respectfully nor be hasty. After learning the truth he will become a steady character.

1103

When their crimes fall on their head, they think of God. When they(fall with their heads under) live headlessly they think not on God. Like sinners do they make a noise as if in (or seeing) a dream, See they this? O Vema.

1104

Words are produced by the thousand (let bags of wards come); yet by well weighing words, they become magic gems. By knowing the composition of words, thou with thy words gain perfection O, Vema!

1105

The mind is of tender age itself. The mind is still youth in all men. Mind witnesses to mind. No decrepitude affects the minds in the world, O Vema!

1106

Though you have gained wealth you may not have got liberality. The wisdom of Brahma Deva is the wisdom of a fool (lit. slave). He gives wealth here and liberality there.

1107

Looking and looking at himself he cannot perceive thee, O God. Looking and looking at thee he would forget himself. He that sees thee is the true saint.

1108

The water poured at the root rises around the root and greatly increases the entire tree. In the same manner the soul pervades the entire body.

1109

Surely the Vedas are all mere contention. Let ashes fill the contentious man's mouth; surely the vanquisher of the Vedas is Vemana. Surely it is our great object to know what is true happiness.

1110

If thou plant a tree carefully but give it no trellis, it will not grow but perish in this world. Thus it is with him who desireth wisdom but can obtain no teacher.

1111

Shall not we cut down the forest of ignorance with the sword of knowledge? Let us not think on ignorance in our mind but look to the places where the light of wisdom is fixed!

1112

Alas none knows intuition (yeriki for everiki). Though thou teach none can understand; by teaching and teaching understanding is produced. Excellent (or divine) is understanding if thou will view it.

1113

Like as the (Parabhruta) cuckoo is reared by the crow, like as the worm comes to life by means of the wasp, thus is it that the fool pretends to be a teacher but cannot bestow perfection (moksha). The nature of the pupil does not depend on the teacher.

1114

If you take a vile fellow and give him wealth he will overthrow even the venerable. Does the dog that gnaws shoes know the sweetness of the sugar cane?

1115

Beasts will not beg of beasts; the race of birds will not submissively ask of their equals. Is he a man who will not bestow when a man asks or is he a woman in the world, O Vema!

1116

What though you have got a *putti* (1600 lbs) or only a cupful of chaff. There is not in it one grain in the world. Trouble only increases in proportion to the store of empty words. The more talk the more trouble.

1117

By want of food they are in distress. How should the wisdom of such mere corpses become fruitless? If you pour water into an unbaked vessel will it remain there in?

1118

He was born in this land and grew up in this land but cannot bestow this land on any one. Alas the man of a foreign country is the king of the world. (Probably alludes to the Musalman Government.) 1119

Why should all wisdom be published? Why should we receive the gifts of a sinner, O sage, ignorantly.

1120

He that quitteth not a faithless friend--is he not a shepherd? (swain fool) Has any shepherd in the world horns (i.e. honour)?

1121

What has a thief to do with good habits? What has a fornicator to do with worship and adoration? What in the world has a palmwine drinker to do with devotion?

1122

This unstable body falls about like a dog; for many days chatters, he gives his body to the fire or to the jackals of the forest.

1123

Your wife is the property of others. Your wealth is the property of the whores. Your body is the property of earth. If you consider them in 'your mind, the virtue (i.e. practice) alone is yours.

1124

If with thy whole heart thou seek and see that, think that it is of wondrous semblance; then shalt thou perceive that it pervades all space and is not of nature divisible.

1125

How should he who is attached to (desires) sin think of the deity. How should the sinner be a teacher? Behold the mind of a fool. Does it know (Had) God?

1126

To cleanse his mouth is a great trouble (nastiness) even to the great saint. Not even a son of Brahma can purify his mouth, But the mouth that speaks the truth is the purest in the world.

1127

First it rises above the water and becomes a sprout; the sprout is itself both husband and son of the earth. The earth is the seed, to both mother and wife

1128

Who are the kings who always being engaged in the earth nourish the world? Whence does the title of great Lord attach to man?

1129

In former time in the world a Boya man, when a tiger roared in the forests, held it to be a cruel beast, and slew it. The sin that he incurred hereby seized the Boysa and whelmed him.

1130

From their birth they continually slay all animals, and become the garden bed of sin. Shall beatitude be attained by evil doers?

1131

Animals that have tails, they get and cut their throats, they break the necks of all the goats of the flocks and as for the rest of the animals they burn and eat them.

1132

They will quit all tasks whatever and the men of the world long (lit. dwell) for the taste of the mouth (eloquence). If you say Devil, the girls are alarmed; all the world has become thus. O Vera I look well to thy words.

1133

Look at your wife. She is shackles on your leg. All your children (in a row) are the rivets. All connections are like to a prison as you consider them closely.

1134

He himself remain sunk in the ocean of love formed by the triple love of wife, offspring and wealth. In what way then should men be able to attain beatitude. When the song is ended we obtain the symphony.

1135

Through those desires that have been wound about us ever since we were children-thus high are we entrapped by the names of relations, called younger sister, elder sister, mother and father.

1136

How many are thy mothers and fathers? How many births hast thou had? Again how many are the places where thou sufferest pain (or live)? The fool knoweth not, this is stable and this fluctuating.

1137

That cannot perceive that life is unstable, thus mad men. They are puffed up here in the earth. All souls are surely in the sight of Yama like as goats bound for sacrifice.

1138

When your father and mother are dead, you and your wife unite and look to building your house agreeably. Like as though a thief already fixed on the impaling post should ask for food.

1139

Increase are decrease, consider, occur to all, however great. The body is not real, if you think on the facts. They cannot know this. What can we say to this.

1140

Through a selfish spirit it is that we say of any one thing, I cannot live (or get on) without this. To have it, but to know you cannot perceive it, go to. This is the bond of the worldly life.

1141

What though we learn and know whence we came and where we go; it is but like the coming or going of sleep. The birth and departure of the soul, these behold, form the divine state and are alone of importance.

1142

All men are bound in the cords of their lusts, shining in their dignity. They cannot sever it with the sword of wisdom.

1143

Who are ye that ye should be able to walk independently of the endless course of time. Relinquish all your idiotic properties and walk, O men in the paths of beatitude.

1144

What has become of all the noble race that lived of all? They might have exalted them in the world. To crush their enemies none has prevailed besides Siva.

1145

Things that are produced from earth we separate from earth and dress them again in an earthen vessel; at what strong love we feel for the earthen vessel?

1146

Vegetables without salt are to the taste vile as (salt ground) barren land. A ruined wretch is he that hath no shoes and the man out of debt is the richest of the wealthy.

1147

The egg in the womb dwells in the body. By the course of breath it pleasantly rambles. This is like austerity in a vine-yard (under a palm tree). When shall he attain bliss.

1148

How is instruction gained? He cannot see the top of his head. It is good to seek him, the deity who dwells on the top of your head. That skilful man who comprehends his head, takes beatitude by violence.

1149

In truth, worth is the source of a faithful intention; devoid of faith thou shalt not attain bliss. What is this we call bliss? Thou art thyself its origin.

1150

Formerly *Boya* Kannappa drew near to the three-eyed god and became beatified. Purity of heart is the root of all acceptable worship.

1151

Time is the effective form of Siva. Time is the duration of God. How shalt a fool know the meaning of true happiness?

1152

By means of a name, a country becomes a holy ground. Thus have stones, through names become kings (i.e., idols). By names have water become all holy streams.

1153

For garden herbs, for spontaneous vegetables, for bran and for empty ears (of corn), those jack asses who for such boons as these have written poems and have become as great as the truly excellent.

1154

When we were born in the womb of our mother at first we not clothing nor shall have at our latter end. Is not it then a joke for us to wear clothing in our intermediate life?

1152

There is no artist in the land nobler than the creator. Draw near with delight to him the lord of all; who is greater than that artist; are men to revile the creator.

1156

If he knows not how to restrain his five senses, and cannot (hold) check the flame of the fire within, and if he has not singleness of heart how shall he regenerate?

1157

He considereth himself the teacher of all the tribes (castes) but knoweth not death, this son of a pariar, when this teacher dies he is vile as the crow that never had a teacher.

1158

He that cannot restrain his mind is in his soul even lower than a pariar, after death hell shall be his fate. O men!

1159

Is not it wrong to call that man living soul who can perceive no beauty in the deity Where is the linga? Where is the Zangam? (i.e., what has such a Zangam to do with the linga).

1160

Relinquish the degraded commerce of excessive sensual delights (Lit. delights of the five senses) and truly become part of the divine self. Let not the internal vision desire the pleasures of eyesights. Call not merely with thy mouth on god, O Vema!

1161

Externally ye suspend the lingam to a number of threads and daub yourselves externally with ashes, yet cannot see that God who dwells externally in all space, 1162

When God ordered the world to proceed by means of death and birth, the name of teacher is attached to him; false is the teacher who knoweth not that his own death is certain.

1163

See these robbers call themselves teachers--void of knowledge, ignorant of themselves--these unprofitable sons of slave.

1164

There is not a single teacher who can show us the (gurutu) truth, not one excellent scholar is there who discerneth the truth. A teacher and a wise pupil are rare as a hare's horns.

1165

Setting up a teacher in even each religion, not even one man hath attained bliss. They worship unblushing teachers.

1166

One is born only to devour food, and perishes, another is born to attain beatitude, and perishes. To attain power another becomes a pariar...

1167

They talk and say there is a teacher in each sect--O ye pariars! ignorant of hidden truth. He that calls himself, dies a crow devoid of instructor.

1168

In the evening the Brahmin performs the religious draughts. The king mounts the sedan, in this earthly dwelling. The cobbler dances a jig. The disease is healed by medicine.

1169

First knowledge, thereby...let not the pious entertain doubts; without the illumination of a lamp shall darkness be dissipated?

1170

Knowing that the body will perish in the ground, yet through great attachment a man nourishes it. Lo! Lo! like as if he should cut off his nee and set himself to drink the blood, 1171

How large this exterior may be. I know not what connection there is between the divinity and this world. In the estimation of the wise how large is the sun, Thus musing they are evidently alarmed. (exemplification of doubt.) ("sunt qui formidive nulla Imbuti spectent") 1172

If rain raineth, the field fruiteth. If rain fall not, it is soon dried up. Thus is the field ordained as sustenance to all.

1173

He that speaketh the truth (tatwa) is to be met with some where in the earth. But he who knows the truth is no where found. If he should exist, he is certainly imperceptible to us.

1174

He who being charitable in his mind considers the hungry guest as God, and without the least heat (displeasure) gives him a mouthful (as much as a nut) of food, this is the man who can cry avaunt to yama (death) and slay him.

1175

Our connections (family) being about us and living in sweet enjoyment, in the midst of them their ruler (the soul) sits. O ye men attain the dwelling of God; there alone is true happiness found.

1176

After you have boiled vegetables, is it possible to pick out the straws? Sense would teach you to gather them before boiling, After you have lost all you possessed where is charity (dharma).

1177

Where trees are produced, fruits also flourish, They must be cut down (or gathered) with a knife. If you dress and eat them, you will know their quality.

1178

While there is still salt and tamarind fruits in the village why dread famine, O farmer! Is there no orpiment? Is there no tin? (That is, I advise you to poison yourselves either with natural poisons or with immoderate quantities of salt or tamarind acid).

1179

If with a mouth defiled with spittle thou meditate on him, does the divinity thereby become spittle (in a thousand ways)? However many persons we name they are not thereby defiled.

1180

He who in the budding of prosperity gives the gifts of a virgin (kanyadan), at the last the region of holiness shall be attained by him. This is the secret of Vedanta.

1181

If seeing one man's wealth and strength, and desiring his gold, thou give him thy daughter (kanya) heaven exists not for thee. He who favouring the poor gives a female to him, what is the use of talking? He is the Parama Siva.

1182

The dowry (or gift in marriage) which is given through seeing and desiring, all possessions and good things perish. A disproportioned dowry produces much profits.

1183

At the time when they give a daughter to a man of wealth, fools exult greatly. It is merely the result of their prayers. Will your pride remain stable?

1184

Though he be devoid of learning, and void of money, if after all even a fool, or dumb, if she be grown you may give her to a favourite connection (bandhu).

1185

He who takes a connection of his own and without reckoning his wealth, looks only to his age bestows the dowry and thus gives his daughter (woman) in marriage, this is the wisest of all.

1186

If you bestow your daughter in marriage looking to wealth, it is as if you gaffe her for a price. The dignified way is to give her to an equal. If thou give her to a poor man, they remain entwined in close attachments.

1187

Giving one's daughter to a rich man is like the water of a well flowing into the sea. But a woman given to a poor man is like watering a lime tree with sea of water, 1188

Through a man's wealth he gets an excellent wife (*punyavati*). Thus a fit husband is also gained by an excellent woman. By the fortune (bhagam) of both, friends and good sons and the eight blessings will be gained.

1189

When a marriage contract (manuvu) is made by a rich man with a poor one, wealth and poverty became thereby united. What then is possession and what is poverty?

1190

Mother, father, friends and relations, and all others will seek and desire a young man. They will give him the girl but not fortune with her.

1191

There is no place that exists not in the mind it is closely united with our acts, if we meditate on God in our hearts.

1192

During his life he doth not restrain his lusts but when death comes, he turns recluse. Without thou quell thy mind, is beatitude attainable?

1192

If thy eye be single, the knowledge shall be one like a man in this earth is united with a woman. Then shall thy interior be full of light like to the lord of the world.

1194

Born in the dark, we grow up in the darkness. Why are we ensnared in the (concealment) darkness of delusion. If thou understand this darkness, this whole world shall appear to thee.

1195

Not seeing the might of time and imagining that this present is perpetual they merely weary themselves. How is it that the men of this world can never discern this noble boon, the lapse of time.

1196

Through worshipping the three eyed in ignorant faith, in former time, Boya Kannappa became a sage. Did this happen through his worship? Wisdom was the cause.

1197

If while we own the error of another we ourselves participate therein, the fortune we enjoy will perish. Is it not enough if water leaks out of a cracked pot (i.e., defect is merely less obvious)? (Olla Ollam melamopraction of pellat) 1198

Shall the amorous, or he that is enslaved to cupidity or for wealth, or that is engrossed in attachment to his family or the stubborn, or he who (makes his face half) turns away his face, see heaven? Though these turn out of the way shall the words of Vemana ever fall to the ground?

1199

By the spread of the passing wind, (water touched by it,) water acquires coolness. There is another secret hidden near to this, if men would understand it (the mind is similarly affected by outward occurrences).

* * *

1200-1215

1200

In this world there is not the blessing of complete happiness they say, how then should that happiness be attained in the next world? If death were not present with us from the first, how should it at last visit us. (Our ultimate good or bad fate is but a continuation of our present lot).

1201

This frail body suffers numberless changes in many ways. Do we nourish and foster it? At last it is given to the funeral flames or to the foxes of the wilderness.

1202

If a soldier skilled in war serves a base master he will disobey and turn again from seeking his favour. He will roam the towns and hamlets like a monkey.

1203

Sand, coals, stones, grass, skin, dirt, sticks, where is the sinner who does not bless his teeth with some of these things.

1204

Will not those who are ignorant of swimming fall into a deep well? How should those who understand swimming fall into the pit, alas, so as to be reduced to powder.

1205

If numerous vessels be placed in one house they are all in various shapes. If this diversity be removed, all will become space.

1206

Why O ye men do ye always think on the body? Cannot ye perceive that the body is perishable? Like to a bandicote caught and dying in a trap.

1207

If thou consider the deity far removed from thee, he shall be far from thee. If thou consider the body as his dwelling he shall dwell therein and if thou hold life to be his vehicle, such men shall remain stable as gods.

1208

Classes and customs vary; but birth is one. Viands differ but hunger is one.

1209

The Sun, Moon, Tusda, Woden (Bhouma), Thor (lit. the teacher, Brihaspati), Frida (sucra), and Saturn--These are signs only but each day is the same.

1210

What is Borax--a substance that is luminous coalesces with metals, uniting them in love. The life is united to the body in a similar manner.

1211

He proceeded from woman and longs for woman. Why all this love of woman and affection for her. He who gives up woman shall gain wisdom.

1212

All fear belongs to the animal body; if fear depart the whole essence shall become the divine spirit. All destruction belongs to the body and all victory to the soul.

1213

Whatever difficulties a man meets within this world, it is not a place that can be instrumental to the attainment of the next world. Then they are not worthy however closely you view them.

1214

How many are they that live on earth, in heaven, and between them; has any one the power to count them. Those who live are indeed those who die.

1215

If God be ours (if the Deity has been attained by us) in even the destruction, we shall rejoice in glorious majesty. He that knows not God shall remain a captive.

* * *

Printed in Great Britain
by Amazon

34879971R00083